In the
WHIRLPOOL

WILFORD WOODRUFF
Member of the Quorum of the Twelve Apostles
and later LDS Church president, Woodruff took refuge
in Atkinville, Utah, during the polygamy raids.
Courtesy LDS Church History Library.

In the WHIRLPOOL

The Pre-Manifesto Letters
of President Wilford Woodruff to
the William Atkin Family, 1885–1890

EDITED BY REID L. NEILSON

WITH CONTRIBUTIONS BY
THOMAS G. ALEXANDER AND JAN SHIPPS

THE ARTHUR H. CLARK COMPANY
An imprint of the University of Oklahoma Press
Norman, Oklahoma
2011

The assistance of descendants of William and Rachel Atkin—especially
Ralph R. and Katherine L. Neilson—in support of this edition of
In the Whirlpool *is gratefully acknowledged.*

Library of Congress Cataloging-in-Publication Data
Woodruff, Wilford, 1807–1898.
  In the whirlpool : the pre-manifesto letters of President Wilford Woodruff to the William Atkin family, 1885–1890 / edited by Reid L. Neilson ; with contributions by Thomas G. Alexander and Jan Shipps.
    p. cm.
  Includes bibliographical references (p.) and index.
  ISBN 978-0-87062-390-5 (hardcover : alk. paper)
  1. Woodruff, Wilford, 1807-1898—Correspondence. 2. Mormon Church—Presidents—Correspondence. 3. Atkin, William, 1835-1900—Correspondence. 4. Atkin, Rachel Thompson, 1835-1903—Correspondence. 5. Atkins family—Correspondence. 6. Polygamy—Religious aspects—Church of Jesus Christ of Latter-day Saints. I. Neilson, Reid Larkin, 1972– II. Alexander, Thomas G., 1935– III. Shipps, Jan, 1929– IV. Title.
BX8695.W55A4 2011
289.3092—dc22

                                    2010030367

The paper in this book meets the guidelines for permanence and durability
of the Committee on Production Guidelines for Book Longevity
of the Council on Library Resources, Inc. ∞

Copyright © 2011 by the University of Oklahoma Press, Norman,
Publishing Division of the University.
Manufactured in the U.S.A.

1 2 3 4 5 6 7 8 9 10

To
Rachel Thompson Atkin (1835–1903),
my great-great-grandmother

*Now Brother William I am not going to address you alone
and leave Sister [Rachel Thompson] Atkin out who has cooked for me
for a year as I tell you we have got to acknowledge our wives or we will be in
a bad fix. I have ate at your table for something like a year with Sister [Atkin]
at the head to serve us and I think we would have been bad off without her
so I must acknowledge her as the lady of the home who has done
me and my family many kindnesses.*

PRESIDENT WILFORD WOODRUFF TO WILLIAM ATKIN, 1890

We are still in the whirlpool.
I don't know how we will come out but trust to the Lord.
PRESIDENT WILFORD WOODRUFF TO WILLIAM ATKIN, 1888

Contents

Illustrations

Preface

President Wilford Woodruff (1807–98) was a historian's historian. Latter-day Saint chronicler B. H. Roberts maintained that Woodruff's voluminous journals constitute one of the most significant records in Mormon history. "Other men may found hospitals or temples or schools for the church, or endow special divisions or chairs of learning in them; or they may make consecrations of lands and other property to the church," Roberts wrote. "But in point of important service, and in placing the church under permanent obligations, no one will surpass in excellence and permanence or largeness the service which Wilford Woodruff has given to the Church of Jesus Christ in the New Dispensation, by writing and preserving the beautiful and splendid *Journals* he kept through sixty-three eventful years."[1] Not surprisingly, many historians of Mormonism have transcribed and published Woodruff's handwritten journals, while other admirers have likewise gathered and put his sermons into print decades after his passing.[2] Woodruff was also

---

[1] Joseph Smith, Jr., *History of the Church of Jesus Christ of Latter-day Saints*, ed. B. H. Roberts, 2nd ed., rev., 7 vols. (Salt Lake City: Deseret Book, 1971), 6:354–55.

[2] For editions of Woodruff's journals, see Wilford Woodruff, *Leaves from My Journal* (Salt Lake City: Juvenile Instructor Office, 1881); Wilford Woodruff, *Wilford Woodruff, Fourth President of the Church of Jesus Christ of Latter-day Saints: History of His Life and Labors as Recorded in His Daily Journals*, ed. Matthias F. Cowley (Salt Lake City: Deseret News, 1909); Wilford Woodruff, *Wilford Woodruff's Journal, 1833–1898, Typescript*, ed. Scott C. Kenney, 9 vols. (Midvale, Utah: Signature Books, 1983–84); and (continued, next page)

an indefatigable letter writer. While serving as a member of the Quorum of the Twelve Apostles (1839–80), president of the Quorum of the Twelve Apostles (1880–87), and finally president of the Church of Jesus Christ of Latter-day Saints (1887–98), Woodruff corresponded by letter with hundreds of LDS leaders and laity, along with members of other faiths. Yet one can count on two hands his individual letters that have been reprinted over the past century. No one made a serious attempt to collect and publish Woodruff's voluminous correspondence, for any time period or on any subject of his life, until now.

Wilford Woodruff, Mormonism's fourth president and prophet, was born on March 1, 1807, in Farmington (Avon), Connecticut, to Aphek and Beulah Thompson Woodruff. Like many other New Englanders of his day, Woodruff was educated in local schools, including the Farmington Academy. His spiritual upbringing centered around the local Congregational church, until he left his family's congregation, together with his father and uncle, in search of primitive Christianity. As a religious seeker, Woodruff eventually moved to Richland, New York, where he cultivated crops with his brother Azmon. There he came in contact with Mormon missionaries Zera Pulsipher and Elijah Cheney, who had been sent by Joseph Smith to evangelize the region. Woodruff was baptized into the LDS Church on the last day of 1833, and once he put his hand to the gospel plow

Susan Staker, ed., *Waiting for the World's End: The Diaries of Wilford Woodruff* (Salt Lake City: Signature Books, 1993). For editions of Woodruff's sermons, see Wilford Woodruff, *The Discourses of Wilford Woodruff*, ed. G. Homer Durham (Salt Lake City: Bookcraft, 1946); *Collected Discourses Delivered by Wilford Woodruff, His Two Counselors, the Twelve Apostles, and Others*, ed. Brian H. Stuy, 5 vols. (Burbank, Calif.: B.H.S. Publishing, 1987–92); and *Teachings of Presidents of the Church: Wilford Woodruff* (Salt Lake City: Church of Jesus Christ of Latter-day Saints, 2004).

he never looked back. Within a year, Woodruff was marching with hundreds of other Latter-day Saints of Zion's Camp fame to Jackson County, Missouri, to help redeem and protect their fellow church members in duress. Proselyting missions to the southern states of Arkansas, Kentucky, and Tennessee followed for Woodruff. In 1836, he returned to Kirtland, and he married Phoebe Whittemore Carter the following year.[3]

Numerous ecclesiastical leadership opportunities resulted from Woodruff's years of dedicated service. He was called to the Second and later the First Quorum of the Seventy (both leading LDS Church councils) and fulfilled additional missions in southeastern Canada and New England. In 1838, Woodruff was named to the Quorum of the Twelve Apostles. The next year, he joined his fellow apostles as a missionary to Great Britain, where he converted hundreds until his departure in 1841. When Woodruff returned to Nauvoo, Illinois, he and his quorum helped Joseph Smith administer the growing church. He was campaigning for Joseph Smith's U.S. presidential campaign in New England when he received word that the founder of Mormonism had been murdered in Carthage, Illinois. In the fall of 1844, Woodruff was appointed to lead the church's evangelism in Great Britain. He remained there until 1846, when mobs in Illinois made it clear that the Latter-day Saints would have to leave their homes in Nauvoo. That summer Woodruff and his loved ones made their way across Iowa to Winter Quarters on the banks of the Missouri River. He entered the Salt Lake valley with Brigham Young and the pioneer vanguard company in July 1847.[4]

Over the next several decades, Wilford Woodruff helped direct the LDS Church (which was, by then, based in Utah) and

[3] Thomas G. Alexander, "Wilford Woodruff," in *Encyclopedia of Latter-day Saint History*, ed. Arnold K. Garr, Donald Q. Cannon, and Richard O. Cowan (Salt Lake City: Deseret Book, 2000), 1361–62.
[4] Alexander, "Wilford Woodruff," 1362–63.

aided in the colonization of the Great Basin region. Because
of his apostolic seniority, Woodruff became president of the
Quorum of the Twelve Apostles in 1880. He would lead the
LDS Church from 1887, when President John Taylor passed away,
until his own death in 1898. Woodruff's presidential administration overlapped with one of Mormonism's most trying periods,
which was fraught with challenges because of the continued LDS
practice of plural marriage and the U.S. federal government's
determination to stamp out this nontraditional and, by then,
illegal family arrangement. Woodruff began practicing polygamy in Nauvoo, as taught by the late Joseph Smith. He married
Mary Ann Jackson (1846), Mary Carolyn Barton (1846), Mary
Giles Meeks Webster (1852), Emma Smoot Smith (1853), Sarah
Brown (1853), Sarah Delight Stocking (1857), and Eudora Lovina
Young (1877) while his first wife, Phoebe (1837), was still living
(see appendix 2). Woodruff, as LDS Church president, would
not announce the Manifesto (suspending additional plural marriages) until September 1890 (see appendix 3).[5]

Decades after mobs drove the Latter-day Saints from Illinois to the Great Basin desert in 1847, the federal government
attempted to eradicate Mormon polygamy. The Edmunds Act
of 1882 and the Edmunds-Tucker Act of 1887 imprisoned more
than one thousand polygamous Latter-day Saints and led to the
near financial ruin of the LDS Church. During the preceding
decades, the geographically isolated Mormons had shunned
America's pluralistic vision while instead integrating their own
religious, political, social, and economic life. Over time, however, the American Protestant establishment coerced the Latter-day Saints to move toward the American mainstream. In
the years that followed, Latter-day Saints were pressured to jet-
tison this earlier way of life in the "Kingdom of God," an era

[5] Alexander, "Wilford Woodruff," 1363–64.

that has become known as "Mormonism in transition."[6] For the time being, however, Woodruff espoused his church's position on plural marriage. As a result, he was forced "underground," or into long-term hiding in southern Utah, beginning in February 1879, by federal marshals roaming the streets of Salt Lake City searching for Mormon polygamists.[7]

While writing the biography of William (1835–1900) and Rachel (1835–1903) Atkin, my great-great-grandparents who pioneered on behalf of Mormonism in southern Utah, I was intrigued to learn of their close relationship and regular correspondence with Wilford Woodruff.[8] The Woodruffs and Atkins became dear friends during the height of the federal government's antipolygamy raids in Utah. As president of the Quorum of the Twelve Apostles and later president of the LDS Church, Woodruff was one of the most sought-after fugitives because of his continued practice of plural marriage, which had been illegal in the territories of the United States since 1862. The Atkins provided him with much-appreciated sanctuary from federal lawmen in their family village in southern Utah during the 1880s. I discovered that my extended family had preserved nearly sixty of Woodruff's letters, which he wrote between 1885 and 1894 to the Atkin family. My distant cousin, Bessie Atkin Doman, donated the originals to the LDS Church History Library in Salt Lake City, Utah, to ensure their preservation years ago.[9] And Atkin family members later gifted a complete microfilm copy of the letters to

---

[6] Alexander, "Wilford Woodruff," 1363–64; and Thomas G. Alexander, *Mormonism in Transition: A History of the Latter-day Saints, 1890–1930* (Urbana: University of Illinois Press, 1986), 14.

[7] See Thomas G. Alexander, "An Apostle in Exile: Wilford Woodruff and the St. George Connection," Juanita Brooks Lecture Series, 1994 (St. George, Utah: Dixie College, 1994).

[8] Reid L. Neilson, *From the Green Hills of England to the Red Hills of Dixie: The Story of William and Rachel Thompson Atkin* (Provo, Utah: Red Rock Publishing, 2000).

[9] Wilford Woodruff Letters, 1885–1894, Church History Library, Church of Jesus Christ of Latter-day Saints, Salt Lake City, Utah (MS 5264).

the Utah State Historical Society.[10] But family members and the staff of the Church History Library have been unable to locate the correspondence from the Atkins back to Woodruff.[11] Still, I determined to make these Woodruff letters more accessible to scholars of Mormonism as well as Woodruff and Atkin descendants because of their tremendous historical value.

Woodruff's pre-Manifesto letters to the Atkin family (1885–90) provide illuminating personal and ecclesiastical details that add color and dimension to his celebrated journals and his published discourses. His missives reveal, as few other documents do, the innermost feelings of an American religious leader who felt forced "underground," or into prolonged hiding, by federal judges and lawmen. Woodruff believed that these government officials were denying him and his fellow Latter-day Saints their pursuit of religious life, liberty, and happiness. The Mormon leader's humanity is laid bare in his letters as he simultaneously curses federal officials for their interference in Mormonism's theocratic kingdom and expresses his love for his own family members and his "adopted" Atkin grandchildren. Like his prophetic predecessors, Woodruff "fought for polygamy as a central doctrine of the church's Kingdom of God theology, but understood its influence on family life and accepted its incompatibility with American society at that time. While his letters are mainly personal and reflect his state of mind, they also contain nuggets of historical value," according to historian David L. Bigler. Woodruff, for example, "reveals that Utah's decades-long struggle for statehood had more to do with the sovereignty of its theocratic form of government than the wish to become a state like others of the Union. He also indicated that he considered the Manifesto to be divinely revealed, not simply a church policy. And he offers signs

---

[10] Letters to William Atkin Family, 1885–1894, Utah State Historical Society, Salt Lake City, Utah.

[11] Ronald G. Watt to Reid L. Neilson, October 25, 2000, original letter in editor's possession.

of a millennial expectancy that may have delayed the decision to make peace with the United States in the hope [that] the Lord's arrival would put His kingdom in charge."[12]

In many ways, Woodruff's letters to the Atkin family expose an interesting feature of religious life for LDS leaders during the plural-marriage controversies. As president of the Quorum of the Twelve Apostles, Woodruff laments being driven into hiding away from friends in Salt Lake City but then relates how wonderful it was to fish and hunt while hiding in southern Utah. Being forced out of the public and ecclesiastical spotlight, many church authorities such as Woodruff enjoyed low-profile existences for the first time in decades during this trying era. They were unable to attend their regularly scheduled administrative meetings or travel constantly to far-flung outposts of Mormonism in the American West. They simply had to hide and wait. Even those LDS leaders and laity incarcerated in prison for marrying additional wives seemed to appreciate the lull in their heretofore frantic ecclesiastical lives. Finally they had time to reflect and ponder on the events whirling around them and their church.

Woodruff communicated many of his thoughts on these topics to the Atkins during these lonely times by letter from his other hiding places in southern and northern Utah during the 1880s or through personal visits to Atkinville. And the fact that Woodruff continued to personally write much of his correspondence to the Atkins in later years, even while serving as church president, says a great deal about the importance he placed on personal relationships. His letters reveal the inner man who valued friendships with leaders and laity alike. Woodruff seems just as comfortable fishing with local Latter-day Saints in Atkinville as he did presiding over the leading councils of the LDS Church in Salt Lake City.

---

[12] David L. Bigler to Reid L. Neilson, Mar. 14, 2009, original letter in editor's possession.

Acknowledgments

I appreciate the individuals and institutions that have enabled me to complete this documentary editing project. The leadership of Religious Education and the Department of Church History and Doctrine at Brigham Young University, including Terry B. Ball, Dennis A. Wright, Arnold K. Garr, and John P. Livingstone, provided research assistants and contributed material assistance for this volume. Many friends, colleagues, and family members reviewed the manuscript at different stages and offered helpful critiques along the way, yet I alone am responsible for the finished product. In addition to contributing introductory essays of their own to this book, historians Thomas G. Alexander and Jan Shipps provided guidance and encouragement from the start of this project. Outside reviewers Ronald W. Walker and David L. Bigler likewise shared their enviable historical knowledge and professional critiques on the manuscript at several points in the publication process. Fellow Atkin family members, including J. Ralph Atkin, Jacqueline W. Awerkamp, Katherine L. Neilson, and Ralph R. Neilson, read over the manuscript and offered invaluable feedback from a family history perspective. My parents, Ralph and Katherine Neilson, also provided a financial subvention to help with the production costs. Susan Staker Oman generously allowed me to adapt her chronology of Wilford Woodruff's life as an appendix in this volume. My wife, Shelly, and children, John, Kate, and Allyson, were supportive throughout the entire process. Publisher Robert H. Clark and the staff of the Arthur H. Clark Company and the University of Oklahoma Press continue to be a delight to work with. Lastly, the Intellectual Property Office and the Church History Library of the Church of Jesus Christ of Latter-day Saints generously authorized me to reproduce these Wilford Woodruff letters and waived their permissions fee. All of these persons and organizations deserve to be thanked and remembered for their generosity and contribution to the recovery of this complicated chapter in Mormon and American religious history.

Editorial Method

B ecause I am both a professional historian and an Atkin descendant, my purposes for editing the letters of Woodruff to the Atkin family are understandably twofold. First, I seek to provide fellow scholars with insightful contextualization and accurate transcriptions of the Woodruff correspondence, which they can use in their own historical work. Second, I desire to make the letters as accessible as possible to Woodruff and Atkin offspring who want to know more about the Woodruff-Atkin relationship but may lack historical training.

To connect with both audiences, I begin this volume with three introductory essays. "A Friendship Forged in Exile: Wilford Woodruff and the William and Rachel Atkin Family" is my attempt to capture the personal trust and familial intimacy that developed between Woodruff and the Atkins in the years leading up to the 1890 Manifesto. Next, historian Thomas G. Alexander offers "The Odyssey of a Latter-day Prophet: Wilford Woodruff and the Manifesto of 1890," a historical overview and analysis of how Woodruff came to the conclusion that Mormonism must discontinue plural marriage and assimilate further into American society. Finally, "The Principle Revoked: Mormon Reactions to Wilford Woodruff's 1890 Manifesto" is religious studies scholar Jan Shipps's examination of how Latter-day Saints responded to Woodruff's policy shift regarding the practice of polygamy. Supplemental resources—including a

chronology of Woodruff's life, charts outlining the families of
Woodruff and Atkin, and the text of the Manifesto—are presented as appendices to help all readers better understand the
life and times of Woodruff and the Atkin family.

The forty-six letters written by Wilford Woodruff to members of the William and Rachel Atkin family between 1885
and 1890 are the heart of this documentary history. Years ago
I traveled to Madison, Wisconsin, to attend the Institute for
the Editing of Historical Documents, a fellowship sponsored
by the National Historical Publications and Records Commission, the University of Wisconsin–Madison, and the Wisconsin
Historical Society. Nineteen of us fellows listened to several of
America's most accomplished documentary editors discuss the
various ways that manuscripts may be prepared for publication. Noted scholars John P. Kaminski, Richard Leffler, Daniel
Feller, Cindy Filer Speer, and Allida Black all offered insightful
sessions on different phases of the editorial process. Then as a
group we debated (sometimes hotly) the merits and drawbacks
of each of the five major methods of transcription: photographic
facsimile, typographical facsimile, diplomatic transcription,
expanded transcription, and clear text transcription.[1] While at
"Camp Edit," my cohort came to appreciate why there is no
such thing as an official or correct way to reproduce historical
documents—each methodology has compelling advantages and
disadvantages. Editors must select the editorial method(s) best
suited for their particular manuscript and audience.

To reach both the historical community and familial descendants, I present Woodruff's correspondence as an expanded
transcription, or liberal representation of the text, with a mini-
mal amount of "barbwire" or extensive editorial apparatus. My
goal is to neither obscure nor inflate Woodruff's educational

---

[1] For an explanation of each method of transcription, see Michael E. Stevens and Steven B.
Burg, eds., *Editing Historical Documents: A Handbook of Practice* (Walnut Creek, Calif.:
Altamira Press, 1997), 71–83.

background as evidenced in his nineteenth-century prose. The future Mormon leader enjoyed an enviable education during his Connecticut upbringing. Like other middle- and upper-class youths in his area, Woodruff attended common schools in Northington and Farmington, Connecticut, until his fourteenth year. Thanks to the generosity of his summertime employer, George Cowles, Woodruff then had the good fortune of enrolling in the Farmington Academy during the next several winters, until he reached the age of eighteen. His school offered classes in the sciences (including chemistry and mineralogy), mathematics (including algebra and geometry), the classics (including Latin, Greek, and history), and other subjects (including natural philosophy and surveying). "An uncommon formal education for a nineteenth-century youth when a few years was the norm," Woodruff's biographer notes, "this experience made him one of the best educated of nineteenth-century Mormon leaders and better educated than any nineteenth-century LDS Church president except Lorenzo Snow, who had attended Oberlin College."[2] Regardless of his exceptional antebellum-America educational background, Woodruff's handwritten letters fall short of twenty-first-century spelling and grammar conventions. Scholars and descendants wanting to read Woodruff's mostly holograph letters can access the originals at the LDS Church History Library or photocopied versions at the Utah State Historical Society, both located in Salt Lake City.

My editorial procedures largely follow those presented in the *Documentary History of the Ratification of the Constitution*, a model for documentary editing.[3] With regard to the capitalization, punctuation, and underlining in the Woodruff holograph letters, I have elected to begin each sentence with a capital letter, as many

[2] Thomas G. Alexander, *Things in Heaven and Earth: The Life and Times of Wilford Woodruff, a Mormon Prophet* (Salt Lake City: Signature Books, 1991), 12–14.
[3] As detailed in Stevens and Burg, *Editing Historical Documents*, 78–79. See Merrill Jensen and John P. Kaminski, eds., *The Documentary History of the Ratification of the Constitution* (Madison: State Historical Society of Wisconsin, 1976), 1:44–45.

lines lacked capitalization. Likewise, I have placed periods at the
end of each sentence in the place of dashes or no punctuation
at all and have altered punctuation occasionally within sentences
to improve readability, in accordance with the *Chicago Manual of
Style* (15th edition). Moreover, I have removed random capitalization and underlining except when Woodruff clearly used them
for emphasis. I also have added editorial insertions in brackets
to help clarify the text, including missing first, middle, and last
names when needed. For example, multiple Emma Woodruffs
are referred to in the correspondence (one of Wilford Woodruff's wives along with several of his daughters and granddaughters were named Emma). And Wilford Woodruff had two other
wives both named Sarah. Moreover, William Atkin's wife and an
older daughter were both named Rachel. Therefore, I have provided women's maiden names as well, for clarification purposes.

Other facets of Woodruff's writing pose an editorial quandary.
For the sake of readability, I have silently changed misspelled
words to their modern-day equivalents, in harmony with *Merriam-Webster's Collegiate Dictionary* (11th edition), *Merriam-Webster's Geographical Dictionary* (3rd edition), and the *Style Guide for
Publications of the Church of Jesus Christ of Latter-day Saints* (4th
edition). I have also standardized the spellings of names of persons and places that Woodruff refers to, so that readers are not
confused by the iterations clouding the original letters. Missing
or undecipherable words are indicated with dashes, as follows:
"— —." Lastly, I have updated the abbreviations, contractions,
superscripts, numbers, crossed-out words, and blank spaces scattered throughout Woodruff's correspondence. Truncated dates
are likewise spelled out. I have also silently deleted redundant
words, lowered superscripts to the main line, and standardized
all headings and dates in the letters' salutation lines. Any crossed-
out words, unless significant, I have not reproduced. All of these
changes have been made in accordance with the widespread
expanded-transcription editorial method. I believe that much
more has been gained than lost through this accessible approach.

Part One

INTRODUCTION

A Friendship Forged in Exile
Wilford Woodruff and the
William and Rachel Atkin Family

REID L. NEILSON

If you ever come to the county come and see me and I will do the same by you.
I would like to go over your place [Atkinville, Utah] once more and see
how things look over the farm and pond etc. I hope you may
prosper in all you do. . . . I pray God to bless you for
all your kindness to all men under ground and above ground.
PRESIDENT WILFORD WOODRUFF TO WILLIAM ATKIN, 1888

The Virgin River basin lies south of the Great Basin and north of the Colorado River. It comprises a region of between nine and ten thousand square miles of southwestern Utah, northwestern Arizona, and southeastern Nevada. The headwaters of the Virgin River lie in the seven-thousand-foot-high plateau of northern Kane County, Utah, and the river eventually debouches into the Colorado River. Where the canyons flare outward, the Virgin River slows and widens, creating pockets of agriculture scattered along its banks. Unfortunately, its waters change erratically throughout the year: a slow stream can turn into a swollen, raging flow of water, sand, and debris, wreaking havoc on downstream settlements and crops.[1]

Euro-Americans first explored the Virgin River basin in 1776, when a Spanish expedition party, under the direction of Fray Francisco Atanasio Dominguez and Fray Silvestre Velez de Escalante, traveled through modern-day Washington County, Utah, during its exploration of the American Southwest. In 1826, renowned explorer Jedediah Smith and his party also passed through the area. Smith and his men followed the Virgin River through the narrows south of St. George (the present route of Interstate-15) into Nevada and on to California. In subsequent years, other explorers, trappers, and traders, including Captain John C. Frémont, toured and mapped the region. Three years after Frémont charted the Virgin River basin, pioneers of the Church of Jesus Christ of Latter-day Saints (popularly known as the Mormon or LDS Church) entered the Great Basin to the north. In 1849, Church President Brigham Young sent Apostle Parley P. Pratt and fifty men to explore the Virgin basin and evaluate colonization possibilities. Pratt was impressed, and he encouraged future settlement. Within several years, LDS missionaries to the American Indians and pioneering farmers began settling the basin of the Virgin River.[2]

In the mid-1850s, the possibility of civil war loomed over the United States, so Brigham Young encouraged the Indian missionaries in southern Utah to try to cultivate cotton—a much-needed commodity that could not be grown in the Great Basin

---

[1] Elwood Mead, *Report of Irrigation Investigations in Utah,* Bulletin 124 (Washington, D.C.: Government Printing Office, 1903), 207–208. For a history of the colonization of the Virgin River Basin, see Andrew Karl Larson, *"I Was Called to Dixie": The Virgin River Basin, Unique Experiences in Mormon Pioneering* (Salt Lake City: Deseret News Press, 1961).

[2] Douglas D. Alder and Karl F. Brooks, *A History of Washington County: From Isolation to Destination* (Salt Lake City: Utah State Historical Society, 1996), 1–51. See also William B. Smart and Donna T. Smart, eds., *Over the Rim: The Parley P. Pratt Exploring Expedition to Southern Utah, 1849–1850* (Logan: Utah State University Press, 1999).

to the north. When the missionaries reported that the long growing season permitted cotton to be raised, Young made plans to colonize the Virgin River basin. In 1857, he called the Samuel Adair and Robert Covington Companies to settle southern Utah and grow cotton. Their ranks mainly comprised families from Mississippi, Alabama, Virginia, Texas, and Tennessee who had cotton cultivation experience. Nearly forty families arrived in Washington, Utah, that April, and they dubbed the region "Dixie." These pioneers endured the summer's blistering heat and were forced to continually rebuild their washed-out dams on the Virgin River. Due to the alkali soil, cotton crops did not completely germinate as expected, resulting in a limited harvest and a loss of enthusiasm. A spirit of frustration and hopelessness overcame many of these early settlers.

Undaunted, Brigham Young still believed that his Latter-day Saints could grow cotton in Dixie. But before the LDS Church launched a full-scale cotton-growing initiative in neighboring areas, he wanted to conduct further agricultural studies to ensure success. So Young called several men to establish an additional experimental cotton farm on the Virgin River, and he selected Joseph Horne as the expedition's leader. After exploring the area, Horne and his men established this agricultural station just south of the junction of the Santa Clara and Virgin rivers, which they named Heberville (modern-day Bloomington) in honor of Heber C. Kimball, a member of the First Presidency, the LDS Church's leading council. Horne and his men survived the mild winter and harvested their initial food crops, then obtained cottonseed from settlers living in neighboring Santa Clara and Washington. On May 6, 1858, Horne's cotton farmers commenced sowing cottonseed in the red soil. That summer the men endured the scorching sun as they cultivated their cotton plants. The Virgin River flooded twice that year, completely destroying the manmade dams and necessitating additional dam construction.[3]

In the spring of 1861, President Young visited the fledgling southern Utah settlements. He concluded that a large infusion of additional Latter-day Saints would bolster the farmers' spirits and firmly establish the cotton mission. Young called over three hundred families on colonizing missions to Dixie for further cotton production in conjunction with the church's October 1861 general conference meetings in Salt Lake City. According to pioneer tradition, the list of families called to settle the southern colonies was read during the fall general conference. Actually, President Young asked for volunteers during the conference sessions and did not get any. Shortly thereafter, the First Presidency drafted a list of assigned colonists. Obedient to their prophet, hundreds of Latter-day Saints traveled south to the Virgin River basin, where they eventually settled St. George in December 1861.[4]

Years later, William and Rachel Thompson Atkin, who had embraced Mormonism in England and immigrated to America in the 1850s, were also called to move from their home in Salt Lake City to help colonize Dixie. They arrived in St. George ready to start a new life in late 1868. The Atkins initially settled within the boundaries of the St. George Second Ward, a local congregation, in the southwest corner of town (approximately 175 West 200 South). There the Atkins built their first crude home in southern Utah by stacking rectangular grass sod in bricklike fashion. Although not ideal, this dwelling was sufficient for that first year in St. George. Fortunately for them, William Atkin was able to replace it with a four-room adobe

---

[3] James G. Bleak, "Annals of the Southern Utah Mission," Book B, 58–59, typescript p. 5, 1957, Dixie College Special Collections, St. George, Utah.
[4] See J. V. Long, "Semi-Annual Conference," *Millennial Star,* Dec. 7, 1861, 779–87.

home the following year. While the Atkins maintained their home in St. George, William and his sons spent time south of St. George farming land they had purchased in nearby Heberville. Over the next several years, the Atkins and other families tried to grow crops in the area. But their cooperative farming company began to unravel as families abandoned Heberville for other nearby settlements. Because William was called to labor as a stonemason on the St. George Temple and Tabernacle, they remained living in St. George proper until both sacred edifices were completed in 1877. Having fulfilled their 1868 mission assignment, the Atkin family was open to new opportunities.

Atkinville, a One-Family Village

In 1877, William and Rachel Atkin uprooted their growing family, packed up their modest worldly possessions, and moved from their home in St. George, Utah, to an undeveloped stretch of arable land on the east bank of the Virgin River eight miles to the southwest. The plateau that the Atkins homesteaded was the last area south of Price and Bloomington where farming was feasible. Thereafter the Virgin plunges into the Virgin River narrows, where the cultivation of crops on a large scale is impossible. One descendant suggests that Atkin and his sons surveyed the region and determined to relocate there while farming in Heberville during the mid-1870s. When the Atkins first decided to homestead the area, they found the desert wilderness to be rough, inhabited only by an occasional Southern Paiute Indian, together with native sage and other resilient flora and fauna.[5] No strangers to the challenges of frontier life, the Atkin parents and children (see appendix 2) constructed a stone house on their

---

[5] Levi Atkin, "This Is the History of My Husband's Grandfather Henry Atkin," TMs (typed manuscript, photocopy), 2, copy in possession of author.

homesteaded property. William Atkin's brother and sister-in-law, Henry and Selena Atkin, as well as his sister and brother-in-law, William and Adelaide Laxton, joined them in later years, thereby pioneering a one-family village, a common living arrangement on the western frontier. "The place where we live is called by our name Atkinville because we were the first that took it up when it had never been used by man that anyone knows and we have made it a beautiful place and me and the boys own it all, about 160 acres," William Atkin stated with pride in a letter to a sister-in-law who remained in Great Britain.[6]

As the extended Atkin families grew, so did their family village. In its prime, Atkinville comprised three limestone homes, storage cellars, livestock corrals, hay and grain stockyards, a granary, and several pigpens and chicken coops. William and Rachel expanded their original limestone home to four rooms downstairs, two of which they decorated with carpet and furniture. Adults and children alike enjoyed a fine organ in the parlor. Most of the family slept upstairs in two large bedrooms. Their home also boasted a large porch, with a balcony deck, flower garden, bowery shed, cellar, additional kitchen, and back porch. William and Rachel further improved their property by planting trees near the front porch for much-needed shade. Their youngest daughter, May, grew a flower garden in front of the house. "There was the peace of isolation, the restfulness of silence, the total absence of neighbors. There was also a sense of ownership," family friend Joseph Walker recalled. "The day's needed doings brought the luxury of wholesome physiological fatigue without weariness."[7]

The physical, social, and spiritual isolation in Atkinville came

---

[6] Grace Atkin Woodbury and Angus Munn Woodbury, *The Story of Atkinville: A One-Family Village* (Salt Lake City: privately printed, 1957), 6–7, 44.

[7] Woodbury and Woodbury, *Story of Atkinville*, 7–9, 13.

with a price: the family village had no public water works. During the spring, snowmelt from nearby Pine Valley Mountain caused the river to swell, which temporarily provided potable water for the pioneers. In the summer, however, the Virgin River resumed its normal low level and nearby sulfur and mineral springs contaminated the water, making it unhealthy. As a result, drinkable water had to be shipped from clear springs to the north in St. George. A related problem was how to irrigate the Atkins' farmland, which was located on a bench above the muddy Virgin River. William Atkin and his sons solved this dilemma by digging a 1.5-mile-long earthen ditch upstream from Atkinville; they then dammed the slow-moving river with brush and other objects to divert the water onto their land.[8] They also benefited from a flowing—but not drinkable—spring located on the north portion of their acreage. Eventually, the water provided from the spring and ditch accumulated and created a shallow pond on the property, inviting a menagerie of waterfowl and animals to claim the pool as their own.

As time passed, William and Rachel Atkin dreamed of creating a park or natural sanctuary, complete with a boating and fishing pond, for the benefit of their children and other pioneers seeking to escape the harsh desert of southern Utah. As parents they wanted their children to settle nearby. "My father's great ambition in going on the farm [Atkinville] was to keep us [children] around him. So he made everything as comfortable and our surroundings as agreeable as possible. . . . He was so successful that the place became so desirable that it became quite a Resort and many of our friends would visit us so much that Sunday it was hard for us to get away from the place," their son Joseph explained. "We would always raise an abundance of

---

[8] Mead, *Report of Irrigation Investigations*, 223. Portions of the Atkinville ditch could still be seen in 2000.

melons in their season which were always free to our friends. We also had a large fish pond with a boat on it. My mother's table was always ready for our friends. In fact our place and parents were very liberal and did all they could to make the place desirable so that we boys would be willing to stay on the farm."[9]

During the 1880s and 1890s, Atkinville became a favorite picnic and recreation destination for local Latter-day Saints. Its popularity grew as word spread throughout the region. Joseph Carpenter, editor of the local *Union and Echo* newspaper, painted a glowing picture of Atkinville: "They have planted and now have growing, numerous cottonwood trees which, within a few years, will furnish them with an abundance of fuel. . . . Mr. Wm. Atkin, of that place, informed us he proposes having a Park and pleasure grounds soon, and in connection with their boating lake, will give pleasure seekers a fine chance to spend a few days in that vicinity."[10] On weekends and holidays, crowds traveled over bumpy dirt roads to Atkinville, where they relaxed under the shade trees, fished and boated on the pond, and ate the contents of bulging picnic baskets. Visitors also enjoyed the Atkins' cold lemonade and ice cream. When the pond froze in the winter, the Atkins flooded its surface to thicken the ice. Then they cut the ice into manageable blocks and stored it between insulating layers of straw in a small cave, thereby providing ice during the summer heat of southern Utah.[11] On at least one occasion, the St. George First and Second Wards gathered for a grand picnic to honor their former bishops. "Ice cream was duly dispensed by Wm. Atkin jr. and was prominent among the cooling facilities of the day," a local newspaper reported.[12]

---

[9] Joseph T. Atkin, "Notes on the Life of Joseph T. Atkin," TMs (photocopy), 3, copy in possession of author.

[10] Joseph Carpenter, "Our Surroundings," *Union and Echo* (St. George, Utah), March 1883.

[11] Woodbury and Woodbury, *Story of Atkinville*, 14.

[12] Joseph Carpenter, *Union and Echo*, June 25, 1896.

A Friendship Formed in Exile

Atkinville devolved into a ghost town during most of the twentieth century and became the site of a master-planned active adult lifestyle community named SunRiver at the beginning of the twenty-first century.[13] Several generations after the Atkins abandoned their "one family village," Dixie locals and historians of Mormonism remember the Atkins and Atkinville more for the sanctuary that they and their isolated homestead provided for Wilford Woodruff during the late 1880s than for the memorable parties they hosted. This is not surprising given that Woodruff ranks as one of Mormonism's most important early converts and pioneer leaders. "A man for his season, Woodruff shepherded Mormonism out of a morass of persecution and isolation. He marked the path which led the Latter-day Saints to come to terms with the separation of the temporal and the spiritual and to acceptance and respectability; and he reclaimed and deepened the reservoir of spiritual water that nourished the Saints through trying times," biographer Thomas G. Alexander writes of Woodruff's contributions.[14]

Beginning in 1879, Woodruff took cover from federal lawmen intermittently in southern Utah, where he also served as president of the St. George Temple between 1877 and 1884. The pioneer outpost of St. George lay three hundred miles to the south

---

[13] In 2000, over five hundred members of the Atkin Family Historical Association dedicated a bronze plaque mounted on a sandstone monument in honor of Atkinville in front of the SunRiver Community Center, located at 4275 South Country Club Drive, St. George, Utah. The historical marker reads as follows: "Atkinville—William Atkin and Rachel Thompson were born and converted to the LDS Church in Rutlandshire, England. They immigrated to America in 1855 and pulled a handcart to Utah in 1859. In 1877, the Atkins moved to this area, which they named Atkinville. In its heyday, Atkinville was the site of three limestone homes. With its boating and fishing pond, it quickly became a favorite recreation destination. Atkinville also became a sanctuary for Elder Wilford Woodruff and other polygamists hiding from federal marshals in the late 1880s."

[14] Thomas G. Alexander, *Things in Heaven and Earth: The Life and Times of Wilford Woodruff, A Mormon Prophet* (Salt Lake City: Signature Books, 1991), 331.

of Utah's capital city, the home of the LDS Church's headquarters. Woodruff moved from safe house to safe house in Dixie to elude government marshals. On January 26, 1885, Apostles Woodruff and George Teasdale, together with bodyguard William Thompson, traveled south from St. George to Atkinville by wagon, a distance of about eight miles. "Visited Price City [two miles north of Atkinville], dined with Brother Atkins, visited his fish Pond and returned home," the senior apostle noted in his journal.[15] Subsequent events make it clear that the outdoorsman-apostle was thrilled to have discovered the Atkin family's fishing pond and hunting grounds. Between 1885 and 1887, Woodruff took regular refuge in Atkinville. Like a diamond fashioned under the pressure of the earth's geology, the Woodruff and Atkin relationship was created under the tremendous weight of the U.S. government's antipolygamy prosecution.

Woodruff remained concealed in St. George under the moniker of Lewis Allen, the name of a Connecticut boyhood friend. The apostle returned to Atkinville in late January 1885 to hunt but was met with disappointment: the Atkin children had set fire to the rushes ringing the water's perimeter. "[They] burned them [vegetation] up all around his pond so there was no hiding places to get the wild fowl or any other purpose," he complained in his journal.[16] Fearing for his safety in St. George, Woodruff for a time took refuge in Bunkerville, Nevada. But by early March he was back hiding again in St. George. For several months, only select confidants were aware of the apostle's whereabouts in southern Utah. In the middle of that June, however, Woodruff attended local Sabbath church services. "The

[15] Wilford Woodruff, *Wilford Woodruff's Journal, 1833–1898, Typescript*, ed. Scott G. Kenney, 9 vols. (Midvale, Utah: Signature Books, 1983–84), Jan. 26, 1885. I have modernized spelling, punctuation, and capitalization for readability. This edition is hereafter cited as Woodruff, *Journal*.
[16] Woodruff, *Journal*, Jan. 31, 1885.

people were very much astonished to see me not knowing that I was in the country," he noted with satisfaction.[17] The following week, Woodruff traveled to Atkinville to go fishing—he caught sixty fish that summer afternoon.[18] Atkinville provided the aging apostle with his favorite outdoor sporting activities, which helped pass the tedium of exile.[19]

According to Woodruff's journals and letters, he relished the opportunities to fish regularly in the Atkinville pond and hunt in the vicinity, as the surrounding Virgin River basin and tributaries were home to a variety of game. The Atkins' manmade pond was stocked with fish from the Virgin River. Although William had planned to import carp for his pond, he was unable to stock them while Woodruff was visiting. During the blistering summer months of 1885, Woodruff undertook numerous hunting and fishing excursions from St. George to Atkinville.[20] The church leader's journals are peppered with details of these outdoor adventures. On August 8, for example, Woodruff, his bodyguard, and two member boys traveled to the Atkin homestead, where they caught one hundred chub and shot three quails and seven rabbits.[21] Woodruff returned two days later and bagged three quails and one rabbit.[22] Early that September, the apostle and his bodyguard returned to the pond, where they secreted themselves in the vegetation to hunt ducks. "I shot 6 ducks, got 4. Thompson 2 ducks," he characteristically documented.[23] The following week, the two men broke

---

[17] Woodruff, *Journal*, June 14, 1885.
[18] Woodruff, *Journal*, June 19, 1885.
[19] See Phil Murdock and Fred E. Woods, "'I Dreamed of Ketching Fish': The Outdoor Life of Wilford Woodruff," BYU *Studies* 37, no. 4 (1997): 6–47; and James B. Allen and Herbert H. Frost, "Wilford Woodruff, Sportsman," BYU *Studies* 15 (Autumn 1974): 113–17.
[20] Woodruff, *Journal*, June 29, 1885.
[21] Woodruff, *Journal*, Aug. 8, 1885.
[22] Woodruff, *Journal*, Aug. 10, 1885.
[23] Woodruff, *Journal*, Sep. 5, 1885.

bread with William and Rachel's family. "I rode to Atkins pond & took dinner with Atkins. I killed 4 quail, 3 ducks, 2 large fowl like snipes, one coal black & one snow white & one large heron."[24] A few days later, the duo showed up for more hunting and fishing. "We rode to Atkins pond & spent the day. We shot 10 wild ducks, 4 rabbits & one large fat crane & caught about 100 fish with hooks."[25] This was Woodruff's first reference to fishing with "hooks," or fly fishing, at Atkinville.

Over the next two years, Woodruff sought sanctuary at the Atkin family village, where his personal safety was almost guaranteed and his favorite outdoor hobbies were plentiful. As president of the Quorum of the Twelve Apostles and a practicing polygamist, Woodruff was one of the most coveted federal fugitives of his time. With lawmen regularly raiding St. George residences in search of polygamists, the apostle required an extra-secure hiding place. The Atkins' isolated homestead in the wilderness southwest of St. George virtually ensured Woodruff's security: nearly a dozen miles of barren desert provided a comfortable buffer for anyone hiding with the Atkins. The wagon roads leading to Atkinville from both St. George in the north and Bunkerville in the south were easily surveyed by Atkin family members for approaching teams or horses. Furthermore, the rugged Arizona Strip—where a man or woman familiar with the land could remain hidden for prolonged periods—lay several miles south of Atkinville.

Woodruff entrusted the Atkin family with his safety, both parties knowing full well that what they were doing was illegal. According to *The Story of Atkinville*, upon seeing an approaching federal marshal in St. George, William Thompson's son Will rode his horse to Atkinville to warn Woodruff and the Atkin

---

[24] Woodruff, *Journal*, Sep. 12, 1885.
[25] Woodruff, *Journal*, Sep. 19, 1885.

family. This started a chain reaction. Young Nellie Atkin ran to the hilltop east of the house, where she scanned the roads for approaching riders. When she spotted the buggy of federal lawmen named McGeary and Armstrong in the distance, she alerted the family. The older Atkin family members then rushed to secrete Woodruff, along with blankets, foodstuffs, water, reading material, and his fishing pole, in a special boat, which they pushed into heavy cattails and rushes that lined the nearby pond's perimeter. Once the coast was clear, William Atkin walked to the pond and signaled with a duck call. When asked if he thought the federal marshals could spot him in the pond from the nearby bluff, Woodruff reportedly retorted "that there were plenty of places to hide where neither the marshals from the hill, the devil from below nor the Lord from above could see his boat."[26]

The Atkin families were honored to have President Woodruff as their guest, despite his fugitive status. "All of us children knew [Woodruff] was in the home and we, as well as our parents, were proud to have our home selected for this purpose, since conditions seemed to require his keeping in seclusion for the time," son Henry recalled. "The situation was explained to us and we were told never to mention the fact of his being here, for fear harm might come to this beloved [future] successor of President Brigham Young [and John Taylor]. We would have stood almost any torture before we would have exposed President Wilford Woodruff, or have had anything happen to him through our carelessness."[27] Likewise, son Hyrum reminisced, "We kids, Nellie, May and I could look some of the officers, who came looking for President Woodruff, in the eyes and say

---

[26] Woodbury and Woodbury, *Story of Atkinville*, 27.
[27] "Life of Henry Thomas Atkin," 5. See also Mabel Jarvis, "Henry T. Atkin Interview," *Washington County News*, July 8, 1937.

we didn't know anything about the man. So the officers would go away."[28] Family friend Joseph Walker added, "It was certainly no small honor, even as it was a heavy responsibility, to have such an eminent man's safety and welfare entrusted to this family. . . . [Woodruff's] residency there lent luster and added importance to the place far beyond anything else that could have happened to the village."[29] The Atkins justified their civil disobedience in terms of ecclesiastical loyalty.

Because of Woodruff's presence and President John Taylor's declining health while "on the underground" in the Salt Lake valley, Atkinville became an important administrative hub for the LDS Church during this time. Bodyguard William Thompson brought the Quorum of the Twelve's mail to Atkinville, where Woodruff regularly wrote his official ecclesiastical correspondence and letters to various friends, family members, and civic authorities. From the Atkins' home, he addressed many of the questions and concerns plaguing the church and its leadership during those tumultuous times. Woodruff shuttled frequently between Atkinville and neighboring St. George to take care of LDS Church business. In late March 1886, Woodruff traveled to St. George to meet with Apostle Heber J. Grant.[30] During their discussion, Grant talked to Woodruff about prophetic succession within Mormonism. From Atkinville, Woodruff later wrote a strongly worded letter to Grant, his junior apostle, filled with reasons why there should be no exception to the precedence of the senior apostle becoming the next church president.[31]

Over time, Woodruff became an honorary Atkin family member. William and Rachel's family even constructed an

---

[28] Hyrum Atkin, "Hyrum Atkin, 1954," TMs (photocopy), 1, copy in possession of author.

[29] Woodbury and Woodbury, *Story of Atkinville,* 26.

[30] Woodruff, *Journal,* Mar. 20, 1887.

[31] Woodruff, *Journal,* Mar. 28, 1887. See Ronald W. Walker, "Grant's Watershed: Succession in the Presidency, 1887–1889," BYU *Studies* 43, no. 1 (2004): 195–229.

extra stone bedroom for the apostle's comfort; it was thereafter known as the Wilford Woodruff Room. Tellingly, the Atkin children affectionately referred to the apostle as "Grandpa Allen" or "Uncle Lemmie," careful to never use the Woodruff name that might give away their family secret. Rather than acting self-important and distancing himself from the daily rigors of pioneer life in Atkinville, Woodruff served the Atkins both spiritually and temporally. That spring the apostle regularly attended family sacrament services in the Atkin home. "I held a meeting with the Atkins family. I had the second lecture in the Doctrine & Covenants read and I made remarks upon it followed by Brother Atkin. We partook of the sacrament," Woodruff noted after one of these weekly gatherings.[32] He also ordained four of the Atkin boys to more-advanced priesthood offices, participated in a family baptismal service, and gathered for family councils.[33]

As an "adopted" family member, Woodruff also provided fresh fowl and fish for the Atkin dinner table and provided his own labor on the farm. Hunting, fishing, and farming were seemingly the apostle's way of doing what he could to reciprocate the Atkins' kindness.[34] The senior apostle welcomed the opportunity to contribute his physical talents. One spring day, for example, Woodruff ventured south to the Arizona Strip to help out with the Atkins' sheep herd. "We rode in a buggy 10 M * 4 on horseback over very steep mountains & hills very rocky & rough to Atkins spring in Arizona where he is keeping his sheep herd," he noted with satisfaction in his journal.[35]

[32] Woodruff, *Journal*, May 22, 1887. The Lectures on Faith, seven theological documents produced by LDS Church leaders in Kirtland during the 1830s, were included in the Doctrine and Covenants from 1835 until 1921.
[33] Woodruff, *Journal*, April 17, 24, May 8, 29, June 3, 1887.
[34] Woodruff, *Journal*, June 3, 1887.
[35] Woodruff, *Journal*, May 9, 1887.

Weeks later Woodruff returned to the Atkins' sheep pastures in Arizona to help save fifteen motherless lambs; he could not pass up the opportunity to shoot three ducks.[36] Later that May, Woodruff also helped shear the Atkins' sheep. "I tied up wool & swept the platform. Brother Atkin kept the shears sharp," he recorded in his journal.[37] Years later, while serving as president of the LDS Church, Woodruff referred to this shearing episode in a letter to William Atkin: "I would like to see your flock of sheep. You did not say what number you have. You will have to get along with the shearing without me this year."[38]

Limited in his social interaction while on the underground, Woodruff forged a deep camaraderie with his Latter-day Saint protectors, including the William and Rachel Atkin family. One wonders what topics they discussed during his visits to Atkinville. What did Woodruff and William Atkin whisper about as they huddled in their willow blind, waiting for ducks and other birds to come within shotgun range? What stories and doctrines did they talk about while they fished? Woodruff may have shared his thoughts about polygamy and the devastating effects the federal prosecution of it was having on the church. We can better understand their friendship from their personal correspondence. On August 18, 1885, Woodruff, still hiding in St. George, received the first of many letters from William Atkin in Atkinville.[39] Between 1885 and 1894, Woodruff and Atkin exchanged dozens of epistles. Fortunately, Atkin descendants preserved fifty-nine missives from Woodruff to the Atkin family, the majority of which are published in this volume.

---

[36] Woodruff, *Journal*, May 3, 1887.

[37] Woodruff, *Journal*, May 21, 1887.

[38] Wilford Woodruff to William and Rachel Atkin, Apr. 26, 1890, Wilford Woodruff Letters, 1885–1894, Church History Library, Church of Jesus Christ of Latter-day Saints, Salt Lake City, Utah. Hereafter cited as Woodruff Letters.

[39] Woodruff, *Journal*, Aug. 18, 1885.

As time wore on, the pressures of confinement and loneliness amplified Woodruff's emotions. In late September 1885, for example, his dear friend William Squires passed away in St. George. Following the burial services, the apostle mourned: "So my friends drop off and leave me, but my turn will come."[40] To overcome his grief and get some exercise, Woodruff rode to Atkinville. "I have lain still so long I am under the necessity of having 1 day's exercise in a week for my health," the Mormon leader explained, "so today Brother Thompson took me over to Atkins pond, 8 miles. I took a boat, went into the rushes & watched for ducks. Brother Thompson fished. We caught 6 ducks, 1 rabbit & a string of chubs. We killed 2 hawks & a turkey buzzard."[41] Atkinville had become a sanctuary for the aging apostle.

President Woodruff continued to defend plural marriage during the 1880s, but he found its outlawed practice to be a great trial for himself personally and for the Latter-day Saints collectively. One of his greatest challenges was his prolonged separation from his beloved first wife of forty-eight years, Phoebe (sometimes spelled Phebe by Wilford Woodruff and other family members). In mid-October 1885, Woodruff learned that she had fallen and injured herself in Salt Lake City. Exiled in southern Utah, the president of the Quorum of the Twelve was unable to assist or comfort his companion. Woodruff spent the balance of October overseeing proxy ordinance work in the St. George Temple, as well as hunting and fishing in the surrounding Dixie wilderness, including Atkinville.[42] But on November 1, Woodruff received an urgent letter calling him home to Salt Lake City for pressing family and church business. Damning the risk of potential arrest, he left his sanctuary the next day and traveled north by buggy, arriving at his Salt Lake City home,

---

[40] Woodruff, *Journal*, Sep. 27, 1885.
[41] Woodruff, *Journal*, Sep. 28, 1885.
[42] Woodruff, *Journal*, Oct. 17, 1885.

where he "found Mrs Woodruff quite poorly."[43] After giving
his wife a priesthood blessing, or healing administration by the
laying on of hands, the president of the Quorum of the Twelve
turned his attention to pressing ecclesiastical matters, including the excommunication of Apostle Albert Carrington for
adultery.[44] He shared these personal trials and setbacks in great
detail in a series of letters to William Atkin.

In November 1885, the personal, legal, and ecclesiastical whirlpool drowning Woodruff continued to swirl—the biggest wave
being Phoebe's passing. He described his wife's final hours to
the Atkin family in an intimate missive: "On the evening of the
9th I had an engagement to ride several miles out of the city to
have an interview with Presidents [John] Taylor and [George]
Cannon but before I left I felt impressed to go and visit my wife.
I did, so at about 6 o'clock I saw she was fading. I laid my hands
upon her and blessed her and I anointed her for her burial, kissed
her, bid her good by and sent my love to my friends in the spirit
world. In 2 hours afterward she was dead." The ominous presence of federal marshals at Phoebe's funeral prevented Woodruff
from attending his wife's memorial service. The Atkins in turn
responded to Woodruff's note, expressing their condolences
over Phoebe's death. "Now Brother Atkin I am happy to be able
to inform you that I have had a happy time with my wives and
children with the exception of the death and burial of my first
wife and I have felt resigned to that knowing that she is far
better off to be at rest than to live any longer in the midst of living and afflictions and persecution," Woodruff wrote. "She has
worried about me ever since I left home and I would rather pass
through the remainder of all my afflictions alone than to have
her share it any longer with me."[45] Woodruff's words convey the

---

[43] Woodruff, *Journal*, Nov. 4, 1885.
[44] Lewis Allen (Wilford Woodruff) to William Atkin, Dec. 13, 1885, Woodruff Letters.
[45] Allen to Atkin, Dec. 13, 1885.

tenderness and depth of affection he had for his wife, as well as the emotional intimacy he shared with the Atkin family.

Still, neither Phoebe's death nor Woodruff's altered living arrangements stemmed the tide of legal pressure on the senior apostle. The day after Phoebe's funeral, U.S. Marshal Edwin A. Ireland stationed himself in front of Woodruff's Salt Lake City home, prompting the apostle's immediate evacuation. For the next six months, Woodruff moved secretly throughout the Salt Lake valley, staying with trusted friends. He also began living with his second wife, Emma, his wife of thirty-two years. By this time, Emma and Woodruff had six surviving children living in Salt Lake City: Emma Minilla, age twenty-five; Asahel, age twenty-two; Clara, age seventeen; Owen, age thirteen; Winnifred, age nine; and Mary Alice, age six. Of these six children, only Mary Alice would ever visit Atkinville. However, all the Woodruff children knew of their Atkin counterparts and contributed short lines in their father's correspondence with the Atkin family.

Hoping to help their apostle-friend, William and Rachel Atkin invited President Woodruff to flee northern Utah and hide with their family in Atkinville during December 1885. But Woodruff declined their offer for the moment by letter: "I am doing the best I know how and then have to trust in God. I don't know that I would be any safer in St. George than I would be at present." He then disclosed, "If the Edmunds Bill becomes a law it looks as though they would search through temple district of course. . . . If they get crowding me too hard perhaps it might be better for me to leave the country than to go to prison or hide with family. I have got much too old to go to prison or hide in the mountains for in either case I could not benefit the people. The nation seems determined to do all in their power to destroy the church and kingdom of God from off the earth. They never will have power to accomplish that but they may have power to distress the Saints until Zion is cleansed and the nations ripe for the sickle which is ripening very fast." On a more personal note, Woodruff concluded by thanking the Atkins for their continued kindness. "Remember me kindly to all your family and especially that little granddaughter [Nellie]. All my family are as well as usual," the apostle wrote. "I attend no parties or public gathering. Cannot [be] seen openly, go nowhere only in the night, but it is like a prisoner's life but better than to be in the pen [penitentiary] for obeying the Lord for he is as unpopular today as he was in Jerusalem."[46]

Woodruff continued hiding with his wife Emma in northern Utah during the first half of 1886. But when he learned that a deputy marshal named Brooks and his deputies were hot on his trail that July, Woodruff and several church leaders immediately fled to the safety of St. George.[47] Weeks later, however, the senior apostle covertly ventured back to Salt Lake City to be with his family. But after enduring prisonlike conditions in the valley for a season, Woodruff decided to again find sanctuary in southern Utah. This time Woodruff determined to have his wife Emma and daughter Mary Alice join him on the polygamy underground. Their other five children remained with relatives in the Salt Lake valley. The Woodruff party concealed themselves at the Thomas Cottam home in St. George that November. The apostle's present exile was made more bearable with his wife and daughter nearby. Eager to host their friend and church leader, the Atkins invited the Woodruffs to Atkinville at the end of November 1886. The men hunted migrating ducks and geese, while the women busied themselves with meal preparation.[48] Two days later, Wilford and Emma Woodruff determined to

---

[46] Lewis Allen (Wilford Woodruff) to William Atkin, Dec. 28, 1885, Woodruff Letters.

[47] Woodruff, *Journal*, July 20, 1886.

[48] Woodruff, *Journal*, Nov. 20, 1886.

move to the inviting safety of Atkinville.[49] They made Atkinville their home on the underground during the end of November and early December 1886.

After two weeks of hiding in Atkinville, the Woodruffs moved back to St. George, where they again hid with the Thomas Cottam family.[50] A few days before Christmas 1886, the Woodruffs and Thompsons returned to Atkinville and shot several ducks, quails, and rabbits for their holiday meal.[51] Despite sharing the joy of the Christmas season in Dixie with his wife and daughter, Woodruff craved personal and religious freedom. That New Year's Eve, he bitterly recorded in his journal, "I spent this whole year in Exile, and had not the privilege of Attending one public meeting or conference and have been deprived of officiating in any of the ordinances of the Church in a public meeting."[52] But the following morning Woodruff, together with his wife and daughter, celebrated the 1887 New Year in Atkinville.[53]

In early January 1887, President Woodruff learned that the U.S. government had passed the Edmunds-Tucker Act, which legislated that privately conducted marriages were felonies, that plural wives were obligated to bear witness against their polygamist husbands, and that the offspring of polygamist unions faced disinheritance. Moreover, the exiled apostle was disheartened to hear that Utah women could no longer vote, polygamist men could not serve on juries or in public positions, that the LDS Church was no longer a recognized corporation, and that the federal government was seeking to seize major assets of the church.[54] At this juncture, Woodruff determined that his wife

[49] Woodruff, *Journal*, Nov. 22, 1886.
[50] Woodruff, *Journal*, Dec. 4, 1886.
[51] Woodruff, *Journal*, Dec. 18, 1886.
[52] Woodruff, *Journal*, Dec. 31, 1886.
[53] Woodruff, *Journal*, Jan. 1, 1887.
[54] Richard S. Van Wagoner, *Mormon Polygamy: A History* (Salt Lake City: Signature Books, 1989), 133.

and daughter should return to the comforts and family responsibilities of Salt Lake City, while he would remain in hiding alone in southern Utah.[55] The Woodruff family spent the next week together in Atkinville, before saying goodbye.[56]

After three months together in southern Utah, the Woodruffs were again pressured to separate. "I parted this morning with my wife Emma & last born child Alice," the apostle lamented. "So I am left alone once more."[57] Fortunately, a lonely Woodruff was surrounded by dear friends such as the families of William Atkin, William Thompson, James Bleak, Thomas Cottam, and John McAllister. Moreover, Atkinville and its hunting and fishing grounds continued to be one of the apostle's favorite places to visit during this trying time.[58] In fact, when Marshal Armstrong arrived in St. George in search of Woodruff in late February 1887, the apostle packed his bags and moved to the safety of Atkinville. "We got 8 ducks," he noted that first day back in hiding with the Atkins.[59] The Atkin family village again provided much-needed sanctuary for Woodruff from February 1887 until June of that year.

In early June 1887, Woodruff traveled to the St. George Temple, where he received confidential word from an unnamed associate, likely President George Q. Cannon, of President John Taylor's impending death. "I was informed that President Taylor was in a critical condition. Legs bloated full. Could not turn in bed. Liable to leave us any day. [Neither] his family nor the public are aware of it. Should he drop off suddenly it will be a heavy blow to Israel. He is calm and composed."[60] The next morning, the president of the Quorum of the Twelve Apostles wrote in

[55] Woodruff, *Journal*, Jan. 15, 1887.
[56] Woodruff, *Journal*, Jan. 17, 18, 23, 1887.
[57] Woodruff, *Journal*, Jan. 28, 1887.
[58] Woodruff, *Journal*, Feb. 14, 19, 1887.
[59] Woodruff, *Journal*, Feb. 26, 1887.
[60] Woodruff, *Journal*, June 8, 1887.

his journal, "I did not rest well. Too much deep thinking to sleep."[61] Upon Taylor's death, it was expected that Woodruff would assume the leadership of the entire LDS Church, a burden he was understandably apprehensive to bear. Woodruff briefly returned to Atkinville to retrieve some of his personal items before moving back to the Cottam home in St. George, where he remained until the beginning of July, although he still visited the Atkins several times.[62] Woodruff returned to Atkinville on July 12, 1887, when he collected the remainder of his belongings and said farewell to the Atkins.[63] President Taylor died on July 25, 1887, while hiding from federal marshals in Kaysville, Utah.

Following President Taylor's death, Woodruff became the leader of the LDS Church: he was sustained as church president in 1889. He continued his correspondence from northern Utah with the Atkins in southern Utah in the years leading up to the 1890 Manifesto. From his Salt Lake City office, he made frequent references to the special times he shared with the Atkin family in his letters. "I want you to give my love and blessing to all your sons and daughter. Alice [Woodruff] enquired particularly about May [Atkin] and Nellie [Atkin] and sent love to all. I expect the ducks on [their] part and the quails will be glad that I am shut up in Salt Lake County," Woodruff wrote on one occasion.[64] In January 1889, President Woodruff acknowledged, "I don't think the ducks or fish in your pond are looking for any more trouble from me. Yet I would like to look at them some more."[65] On another occasion, Woodruff expressed his gratitude to the Atkin family, especially the matriarch, Rachel.

---

[61] Woodruff, *Journal*, June 9, 1887.

[62] Woodruff, *Journal*, July 2, 8, 9, 1887.

[63] Woodruff, *Journal*, July 12, 1887.

[64] Lewis Allen (Wilford Woodruff) to William and Rachel Atkin, Aug. 7, 1887, Woodruff Letters.

[65] Lewis Allen (Wilford Woodruff) to William and Rachel Atkin, Jan. 30, 1889, Woodruff Letters.

"Now Brother William I am not going to address you alone and leave Sister [Rachel Thompson] Atkin out who has cooked for me for a year as I tell you we have got to acknowledge our wives or we will be in a bad fix. I have ate at your table for something like a year with Sister [Atkin] at the head to serve us and I think we would have been bad off without her so I must acknowledge her as the lady of the home who has done me and my family many kindnesses," Woodruff wrote. "I cannot forget the many kindnesses and hours of comfort I have received in that stone room built for my benefit and I would like to spend a few more hours there if I had a chance."[66]

It should be noted that Atkinville became and remained a safe house for Mormon polygamists such as Woodruff because William and Rachel did not practice plural marriage themselves. The Atkins apparently felt that they were building Mormondom in their own way by providing this refuge for practicing polygamists. Rachel's sentiments about plural marriage and William's potential involvement have long been retold by Atkin family members.

> Rachel spent long hours cooking for [the polygamists] while they fished and hunted, and since she felt that she was assisting in promoting the work of the Lord here on earth and was innately a most hospitable person, she accepted the extra work with little if any murmuring or complaining.
>
> However, the tradition continues, she felt that her hospitality and forbearance had been stretched to the breaking point one day, when some of these harassed brethren, hearing that the U.S. marshals were in St. George, decided to do some "fishing" at Atkinville. William was immediately dispatched to the garden for vegetables and two of the boys were sent to rob the rooster of three or four fat pullets from his harem to furnish fried chicken for the visiting Mormon polygamists.

---

[66] Wilford Woodruff to William and Rachel Atkin, Apr. 26, 1890, Woodruff Letters.

While Rachel was in her very warm kitchen preparing dinner, she overheard the brethren telling William of the trials that following God's laws entailed when they were in conflict with those made by man. Now and then Rachel thought she detected a sour note in the recital. Later she heard one of them tell William that it was not fair that he, her William, who had not complied with the law of patriarchal marriage, should be allowed to prosper and live in peace and comfort with his family while they were sacrificing so much for the Lord's cause.

When he went on, with the support of the other brethren, to urge her William to take another wife, her Irish temper flared, there was a crash of breaking china and before those bewildered elders realized what was happening she stood in the doorway, the personification of outraged womanhood, and with the sizzling chicken behind her, proceeded to roast those meddlesome men in no uncertain terms. In brief, according to family tradition, she told them that she had heretofore been willing to give them the hospitality and protection of her home, but if they could not hold their meddling tongues they would no longer be welcome. As for William, he could get another wife if he wanted but, and she used the age old threat, as soon as No. 2 stepped foot over her threshold, she, Rachel, would step out and go back to England where he would never see or hear from her again. She meant it and William knew she did.[67]

Although we know Rachel's position on the practice of plural marriage, how did William feel? Did he experience any resentment toward his wife? What pressures did he feel, and how did this affect their relationship? These questions are unanswerable.

---

[67] Woodbury and Woodbury, *Story of Atkinville,* 33. Grace Woodbury shared another variation during an Atkin family reunion: "One day after the church authorities had called a meeting of some of the prominent townsmen and asked them to take another wife, Grandpa [William] came home and told Grandma [Rachel] about it. She carefully threw a few kitchen utensils around and then said, 'Now bring the hussy home if you want to.' He didn't and they lived happily ever after." See "The Atkin Reunion of March 23 and 24, 1951," TMs (photocopy), 2. Copy in possession of author.

The fact remains that, despite ecclesiastical pressures and formal pronouncements by church leaders, William and Rachel did not enter into polygamy, even while aiding its practitioners.[68] The Atkins were not alone in their decision; the percentage of practicing polygamous adults varied by Mormon community. During the decade that Woodruff and other polygamists made Atkinville their sanctuary, over 38 percent of worthy Latter-day Saint households in St. George were involved in plural marriage, according to historian Larry M. Logue.[69]

At any rate, Atkinville retained its status as an open sanctuary for many of these polygamists on the underground. Notable Latter-day Saints who hid in Atkinville include George Q. Cannon, David H. Cannon, James Andrus, Casper Bryner, William Thompson, James Bleak, and John D. T. McAllister.[70] In fact, President Woodruff once enclosed several letters for brethren hiding in Atkinville in a letter to William Atkin. "I received a Letter from Brother McAllister and I judged He was at your

---

[68] There was considerable ecclesiastical pressure on Mormon men and women to enter into plural marriage during the 1870s and 1880s. On many occasions, contemporary church leaders stressed the need for worthy male members to take additional wives. In 1875, the Atkins' beloved apostle Woodruff stated, "We have many bishops and elders who have but one wife. They are abundantly qualified to enter the higher law and take more, but their wives will not let them. Any man who permits a woman to lead him and bind him down is but little account in the church and Kingdom of God." Wilford Woodruff, *Wilford Woodruff, Fourth President of the Church of Jesus Christ of Latter-day Saints: History of His Life and Labors as Recorded in His Daily Journals,* ed. Matthias F. Cowley (Salt Lake City: Deseret News, 1909), 490. On April 26, 1884, Atkin family friend Charles L. Walker attended a special St. George priesthood meeting and listened to President John Taylor and apostles George Q. Cannon and Moses Thatcher speak on a variety of subjects. "Pres. George Q Cannon said He did not feel like holding up his hand to sustain anyone as a presiding officer over any portion of the people who had not entered into the Patriarchal order of Marriage," Walker noted. William Atkin likely was in attendance. Andrew Karl Larson and Katharine Miles Larson, eds., *Diary of Charles Lowell Walker,* 2 vols. (Logan: Utah State University Press, 1980), 2:629.

[69] Larry M. Logue, *A Sermon in the Deseret: Belief and Behavior in Early St. George, Utah* (Urbana: University of Illinois Press, 1988), 49.

[70] Woodbury and Woodbury, *Story of Atkinville,* 32. See Wilford Woodruff to William Atkin, Apr. 23, 1888, Woodruff Letters.

Home and perhaps several other Brethren and so I have written several Letters and enclosed direct to you which I wish you to Distribute when you have a Chance as they may be with you and if they are not send them when you have a Chance," Woodruff wrote. "It seems that you was not inspired any to[o] soon to build that stone room that I occupied as it may accommodate a number of men."[71] Although Woodruff never returned to Atkinville after 1887, the family village remained a place of refuge for other LDS polygamists in hiding.

AFTERMATH

On September 24, 1890, President Wilford Woodruff issued the Manifesto, ushering in the end of Mormon polygamy. He mailed the Atkins a copy of the bombshell declaration that November, two months after LDS Church leaders had formally distributed the pronouncement to the press in Salt Lake City.[72] About that same time, after thirteen years in Atkinville, William and Rachel Atkin together with several children moved back to the comforts and conveniences of St. George, where they remained until their deaths. Family historians Grace and Angus Woodbury note that "when William and Rachel moved away, the cohesive forces that made and kept Atkinville a profitable family project [were] lost."[73] One by one, William and Rachel's sons and daughters, many of them married, left Atkinville. John Peter and his wife, Annie Walker, relocated to St. George with their infant daughter, Grace. Henry and his wife, Sara Jane Ellicock, remained about one more year until they, too, followed suit and abandoned the family homestead. George and his new bride, Caroline Brady, moved into Henry's

---

[71] Wilford Woodruff to William Atkin, Apr. 4, 1888, Woodruff Letters.
[72] Wilford Woodruff to William Atkin, Nov. 19, 1890, Woodruff Letters.
[73] Woodbury and Woodbury, *Story of Atkinville*, 34.

vacant home, where they remained for a season until they were also drawn to St. George. Eventually, Heber and his wife, Emily Pearce, and Hyrum and his wife, Elizabeth McAllister, also left the family farm. An era had ended for William and Rachel Atkins' one-family village.

Between 1891 and 1894, President Woodruff in Salt Lake City and the Atkin family in St. George continued their correspondence. Woodruff wrote an additional dozen letters to his dear friends in southern Utah. William and Rachel Atkin continued to inform Woodruff of what was happening with their growing extended family, including their move to the heart of Dixie. "I was pleased to learn that you have got a home in St. George. I hope it will prove a benefit to you," Woodruff wrote with interest.[74] In subsequent years, the Atkins shared their grief over the unexpected death of their son John Peter, husband and father of three young children. William related the sad news in a letter to Woodruff, who had recently suffered from deaths in his own family. "I received you[r] kind letter of February 1 and feel to deeply sympathize with you in the loss of your son John, but above all other people as Saints of God we shall meet together in the family organization in the morning of the first resurrection to commence laboring in our second estate," Mormonism's prophet responded in comforting his friend.[75] Woodruff shared with the Atkins that his older brother, Thompson, had likewise recently passed away, leaving him alone as his parents' only living child. His empathy was born of personal suffering resulting from the loss of his own loved ones. Woodruff understood the pain the Atkins were suffering and communicated his love in response.

Personal developments and family health concerns became the overriding theme of the Woodruff-Atkin continued corres-

[74] Wilford Woodruff to William and Rachel Atkin, Jan. 15, 1891, Woodruff Letters.
[75] Wilford Woodruff to the William Atkin Family, Feb. 12, 1894, Woodruff Letters.

pondence through 1894, when their letters end (or were simply discarded) without explanation. Once again, Woodruff's intimate missives offer historians and family members little-known details about the Mormon prophet's life. In March 1891, Woodruff confided to the Atkins that he had been so sick for the previous three months that he had not been able to attend worship services or his administrative meetings, a great trial to him as president of the LDS Church.[76] A month later, he disclosed that he had nearly died from his lingering illness.[77] In July 1891, Woodruff shared that after another long bout of debilitating sickness, he had fallen and, in his own words, "struck my forehead on a plank that nearly knocked a hole in my head."[78] The following January, Woodruff was still plagued by a colic that would not leave him alone. "We have had a great many deaths of aged people during the past year. And I feel that the Lord has preserved me in a wonderful manner," President Woodruff wrote the Atkins. He then shared the sad news that six of his children and grandchildren were suffering from scarlet fever and that his contemporaries were dying at an alarming rate. "I want to live to see the temple finished in S[alt] L[ake] C[ity] and assist in the dedication, then I will be willing to go home [to God]," Woodruff concluded of his own mortality.[79] He would live five years beyond the 1893 opening of the Salt Lake Temple. Woodruff's letters were peppered with accounts of his children's health challenges and misfortunes, including accounts of his son David being nearly crippled after being kicked in the leg by a horse and his son Owen's lung problems.[80]

[76] Wilford Woodruff to William and Rachel Atkin, Mar. 27, 1891, Woodruff Letters.

[77] Wilford Woodruff to the William Atkin Family, Apr. 28, 1891, Woodruff Letters.

[78] Wilford Woodruff to William Atkin, July 15, 1891, Woodruff Letters.

[79] Wilford Woodruff to William and Rachel Atkin, Jan. 7, 1892, Woodruff Letters.

[80] Wilford Woodruff to William Atkin et al., Jan. 15, Apr. 28, Aug. 25, 1891, Woodruff Letters.

Over the years, President Wilford Woodruff and the Atkin family drew strength from one another as they shared their joys and trials with an intimacy that is emotionally moving to read and difficult to find in heretofore published sources. Woodruff passed away in 1898; William and Rachel Atkin both followed suit within five years. While hiding in the deserts of southern Utah for his practice of plural marriage, Woodruff was fed not by ravens, like biblical Elijah, but rather by Latter-day Saint families who loved him dearly, including the household of William and Rachel Atkin.[81] And Woodruff repaid their benevolence by sharing with the Atkins the confidential details of his personal and ecclesiastical life for a decade while a political, financial, and social whirlpool swirled around him and his church. A line of Woodruff's correspondence to the Atkins captures their relationship: "I pray God to bless you for all your kindness to all men under ground and above ground."[82] Theirs was a friendship forged in exile.

---

[81] Thomas G. Alexander, "An Apostle in Exile: Wilford Woodruff and the St. George Connection," Juanita Brooks Lecture Series, 1994 (St. George, Utah: Dixie College, 1994), 17.

[82] Wilford Woodruff to William Atkin, Apr. 4, 1888, Woodruff Letters.

The Odyssey of a Latter-day Prophet

Wilford Woodruff and the Manifesto of 1890

Thomas G. Alexander

On September 24 and 25, 1890, eighty-three-year-old Wilford Woodruff, prophet, seer, revelator, and president of the Church of Jesus Christ of Latter-day Saints, met with three of the Quorum of Twelve and his counselors to discuss "an important Subject."[1] Writing about the experience in his diary, he said, "[I have] arived at a point in the History of my life as the President of the Church of Jesus Christ of Latter Day Saints whare I am under the necessity of acting for the Temporal Salvation of the Church. The United State Governmet has taken a Stand & passed Laws to destroy the Latter day Saints upon the

This essay is an expanded version of Thomas G. Alexander, "The Odyssey of a Latter-day Prophet: Wilford Woodruff and the Manifesto of 1890," *Journal of Mormon History* 17 (1991): 169–206.

[1] Wilford Woodruff, *Wilford Woodruff's Journal, 1833–1898, Typescript*, ed. Scott G. Kenney, 9 vols. (Midvale, Utah: Signature Books, 1983–85), 9:109–112. Hereafter cited as Woodruff, *Journal*. Note to the reader: Unlike the previous essay and the letters in part 2 of this volume, spelling, capitalization, and punctuation of quoted material in this essay are as in the original. [2] Woodruff, *Journal*, 9:112.

Subjet of poligamy or Patriarchal order of Marriage. And after Praying to the Lord & feeling inspired by his spirit I have issued . . . [a] Proclamation which is sustained by my Councillors and the 12 Apostles."[2]

The proclamation, which he labeled an "Official Declaration," was addressed "To whom it may Concern." In the proclamation, or manifesto, Woodruff denied that the church had continued to solemnize plural marriages. Indicating that because the Supreme Court had declared constitutional the laws forbidding polygamy, he intended to "submit to those laws and to use [his] influence with the members of the Church . . . to have them do likewise." He denied that the church encouraged members to enter polygamy, and he insisted that church leaders had "promptly reproved" those elders who had done so.[3]

In issuing this declaration, Woodruff and the leadership acknowledged a major change in practice in the church.[4] Possibly as early as 1831 and at least by 1841, Joseph Smith had begun to enter plural marriage clandestinely. Other leaders followed. Officially acknowledging polygamy in 1852, many Mormons considered such marriages a divinely sanctioned responsibility for those who expected the richest blessings of the Lord. By 1890, more than one thousand priesthood holders had suffered

---

[3] For general studies of the issuance of the manifesto, see Henry J. Wolfinger, "A Reexamination of the Woodruff Manifesto in the Light of Utah Constitutional History," *Utah Historical Quarterly* 39 (Fall 1971): 328–49; Howard R. Lamar, "Statehood for Utah: A Different Path," *Utah Historical Quarterly* 39 (Fall 1971): 308–27; Kenneth W. Godfrey, "The Coming of the Manifesto," *Dialogue: A Journal of Mormon Thought* 5 (Autumn 1970): 11–25; S. George Ellsworth, "Utah's Struggle for Statehood," *Utah Historical Quarterly* 31 (Winter 1963): 60–69; Gordon C. Thomason, "The Manifesto Was a Victory!" *Dialogue* 6 (Spring 1971): 37–45; and Jan Shipps, "The Principle Revoked: A Closer Look at the Demise of Plural Marriage," *Journal of Mormon History* 11 (1984): 65–77.

[4] For general studies of plural marriage, see Kathryn M. Daynes, *More Wives Than One: The Transformation of the Mormon Marriage System, 1840–1910* (Urbana: University of Illinois Press, 2001); Richard S. Van Wagoner, *Mormon Polygamy: A History* (Salt Lake City: Signature Books, 1986); and Jessie L. Embry, *Mormon Polygamous Families: Life in the Principle* (Salt Lake City: University of Utah Press, 1987).

imprisonment as a result of their refusal to abandon the principle; judges had sent many women to prison for declining to testify against their husbands in such cases.

Woodruff himself had vigorously supported the principle. Married to Phoebe Whittemore Carter in 1837, he was sealed to his second wife in 1846, and during the 1850s, he added four more wives to his family. The marriage to his second wife, Mary Ann Jackson, ended in divorce, and his third wife, Mary Giles Meeks Webster, died shortly after their marriage in 1852. Phoebe died in 1885. In 1890, he still had three living wives: Emma Smith and Sarah Brown, whom he had married on the same day in March 1853, and Sarah Delight Stocking, called Delight, whom he married early in 1857 during the Mormon Reformation.[5]

What led Woodruff to issue the Manifesto? The revelation and subsequent change in policy resulted, I believe, from a spiritual, physical, and psychic odyssey that ended shortly after Woodruff's return from California in September 1890. In the process, the president's attitude changed from apocalyptic belligerency to reluctant cooperation as he and the Mormons moved through a psychic watershed, transforming themselves from persecuted outsiders and sectarians to members of a prominent American church that became one of the fastest-growing religious traditions in the world.[6]

Woodruff's odyssey started at least a decade before the Manifesto. After the Supreme Court decision in the George Reynolds case, from February 1879 through early 1880, United States marshals kept then–St. George Temple president Woodruff

---

[5] For a discussion of the reformation, see Paul H. Peterson, "The Mormon Reformation," Ph.D. dissertation, Brigham Young University, 1981.

[6] For a discussion of the Mormons as outsiders, see R. Laurence Moore, *Religious Outsiders and the Making of America* (New York: Oxford, 1986). For a discussion of the LDS Church as a new religious tradition, see Jan Shipps, *Mormonism: The Making of a New Religious Tradition* (Urbana: University of Illinois Press, 1985).

on the run in Nevada, New Mexico, and particularly northern Arizona.[7]

January 26, 1880, found him at a sheepherders' camp in the wilderness of the San Francisco Mountains east of the Little Colorado River.[8] Surrounded by the harsh solitude of a high-country winter, he spent the day reading letters from relatives and friends and ruminating over a series of anti-Mormon lectures. He awoke "about Midnight," full of the Spirit of the Lord, and he received a revelation, which he committed to paper the next day.[9]

Several themes predominated in the wilderness revelation. The message emphasized the imminence of the apocalypse and Christ's second coming, the judgments of God upon the nation, the divinity of plural marriage, the need for the Saints to remain pure and blameless, the power of the Lord in protecting the Saints in the building of their temples, and the Lord's approval of the labors of the Twelve.

Linking the imminent apocalypse to the Saints' persecutors, the message identified those targeted for the Lord's wrath. In a comprehensive list, the text named the president of the United States; members of the Supreme Court, the cabinet, the Senate, and the House; the governors of several states and territories; judges and officials; and others. The revelation said the Lord would pour out his judgment upon "that Nation or House or people, who seek to hinder my People from obeying the Patriarchal Law of Abraham which leadeth to a Celestial Glory which has been revealed unto my Saints through the mouth of my servant Joseph."

---

[7] For the case, see *Reynolds v. United States*, 98 U.S. 145 (1879). He remained at the camp until the decision in the John Miles case allowed polygamists relative freedom of movement. Woodruff knew of Miles's conviction, sentence, and appeal, but his journal does not record the success of the appeal. Woodruff, *Journal,* 7:491. For the Miles case, see *U.S. v. Miles*, 103 U.S. 304 (1880).

[8] The events surrounding the revelation are given in Woodruff, *Journal,* 7:546–47. The text of the revelation and prayer are recorded in ibid., 615–25.

[9] Woodruff, *Journal,* 7:546.

Moreover, the revelation instructed Woodruff to call upon the Twelve to offer a testimony in innocence against those who had persecuted the Saints. The message called upon the apostles to cleanse their feet with pure water as a witness to the Lord, to clothe themselves in "the Robes of the Holy Priesthood," and to bear a testimony through prayer against their persecutors. The church leaders gathered in a prayer circle on January 19, 1881, and did as they had been commanded.[10]

At the October 1880 Conference, the apostles had agreed to reorganize the First Presidency. Sustaining John Taylor as president, they called George Q. Cannon and Joseph F. Smith as his counselors and Woodruff as president of the Quorum of Twelve. As leader of the apostles, in addition to presiding over the church's second governing quorum, Wilford stood next in line for its presidency.

As federal officials increased the pressure on the Latter-day Saints during the 1880s, the church leadership sought to avoid the burdens of the various laws. On March 24, 1882, the day that President Chester A. Arthur signed the Edmunds Act, Woodruff met with the First Presidency, and they agreed to counsel

[10] Woodruff left the list out of his journal, and I have not seen the completed list. Woodruff, *Journal*, 7:624. Returning to Salt Lake in time for the 1880 April Conference, he presented his revelation to the Twelve for their approval. On April 22, the apostles received the revelation "as the word of the Lord," and on January 19, 1881, those members of the Twelve, the First Presidency, and the Presiding Bishopric within reasonable traveling distance, together with the patriarch to the church, gathered in a prayer circle. Even Charles C. Rich, debilitated from a recent stroke, and Orson Pratt, enfeebled by an advanced case of diabetes, met with their brethren. Most conspicuous by their absence were George Q. Cannon, then representing Utah in Congress, and Brigham Young, Jr., Moses Thatcher, Erastus Snow, and John W. Taylor of the Twelve, all of whom were away on assignments. Those present washed their feet "against Our Enemies and the Enemies of the Kingdom of God" as commanded. Keeling at the altar, John Taylor presented Woodruff's written prayer effecting the purposes of the revelation and containing a list of names of those who had "made war against Thee and thy kingdom and thine anointed ones." The prayer called upon the Lord to "protect thy Church, thy Kingdom and thy people from the Power of the wicked" and asked that He inhibit the nation from preventing "thy Saints from keeping thy Commandments, from building the Temples of our God and redeeming Our dead." Woodruff, *Journal*, 8:6–7. The full text of the prayer is found in ibid., 7:621–25.

"the brethren to live with but one wife under the same Roof."[11] Nevertheless, in November 1882, the brethren concluded that they "could not swap . . . the Kingdom of God or any of its Laws or Principals for a State Governmet."[12]

After the passage of the Edmunds Act, between 1882 and early 1885, practicing polygamists stood in the eye of a hurricane. The decision in the Miles case had virtually halted prosecution under the Morrill Act, and the government had yet to work out a systematic means of arresting and prosecuting Edmunds Act violators. Thus, Woodruff and the other church leaders continued with their duties. Woodruff continued to serve as St. George Temple president and to advise on the construction of new temples in Manti and Logan.

In August 1884, the eye of the storm began to pass, and the hurricane soon descended on the Utah community. As advance agent of the storm's fury, Charles S. Zane of Illinois rode into Utah to assume the posts of chief justice of the Utah Territorial Supreme Court and judge of the third judicial district, centered in Salt Lake City. Working with U.S. Attorney Charles S. Varian, who pressed for grand jury indictments, and U.S. Marshal Edwin A. Ireland and his deputies, who scoured the country looking for cohabs, Zane and his fellow judges began to conduct systematic prosecutions and convictions, which filled the territorial penitentiary in Sugar House with unrepentant polygamists.[13]

This raid sent Wilford Woodruff, John Taylor, George Q. Cannon, Joseph F. Smith, and others underground. Woodruff hid out in the Salt Lake Seventeenth Ward meetinghouse;

---

[11] Woodruff, *Journal*, 7:92. The Edmunds Act defined the offense of unlawful cohabitation, disfranchised polygamists, and placed Utah Territory's election machinery in the hands of the Utah Commission.

[12] Woodruff, *Journal*, 8:133.

[13] For a discussion of Zane's activities, see Thomas G. Alexander, "Charles S. Zane: Apostle of the New Era," *Utah Historical Quarterly* 34 (fall 1966): 290–314.

wrote to Sarah, Emma, and Delight; blessed Phoebe; then left for St. George on January 17, 1885.[14]

He remained in St. George under the name of Lewis Allen, a boyhood friend from Connecticut, until November 1885, when John Taylor called him back to Salt Lake.[15] In St. George, he conducted temple sessions, visited conferences in southern Utah and southeastern Nevada, hunted ducks, fished, and farmed.

Although he returned to Salt Lake in November 1885 to attend a clandestine meeting of the Twelve called to consider the fellowship of two apostles, for Woodruff his return bore a much deeper anguish. On November 9, he risked a visit to Phoebe. His wife had suffered a severe attack of "chills" about a month before, and during her sickness she had fallen and split her scalp. When Woodruff arrived, she lay on the verge of death. Recognizing Phoebe's hopeless condition, Woodruff blessed her and "anointed her for her burial."[16] She died a few hours later.

Unable to attend the November 12 funeral for fear of arrest, Woodruff hid at the president's office on South Temple and watched through the windows while friends and family conducted her last rites and accompanied her remains to the cemetery. As the funeral cortege passed, he reflected that he was "passing through a strange Chapter in the history of my life."[17]

Phoebe's death changed Wilford's life. He made arrangements for the disposition of his two houses in Salt Lake City and moved his belongings to Emma's house, about six miles south of the city in Farmer's Ward. After that, he alternated between living on the farm with Emma, staying with friends, living in

---

[14] Woodruff, *Journal,* 8:298–99.

[15] Woodruff, *Journal,* 8:341.

[16] Woodruff, *Journal,* 8:342. The two were Albert Carrington, who was excommunicated for adultery, and John W. Young, an apostle though not a member of the Twelve, who was tried for neglect of duty and given time to mend his ways.

[17] Woodruff, *Journal,* 8:343.

St. George, and, after his call as president of the church, living in the Second Empire Gardo House on South Temple.[18]

Throughout these trials, Woodruff had not budged from the defiant and apocalyptic attitude evident in the wilderness revelation. In various writings in 1885, 1886, and 1887, he emphasized his continuing anticipation of God's imminent judgments upon the nation. On January 13, 1887, as the U.S. House of Representatives passed the Edmunds-Tucker Act, he expected that the approval of that bill would seal Congress's "condemnation" and lay "the foundation for the overthrow & final destruction of the United States government."[19]

During early 1887, John Taylor became increasingly infirm, and members of the Twelve began to contemplate a succession in the presidency. Responding to an inquiry from Heber J. Grant, Wilford expressed his strong conviction that the president of the quorum should automatically succeed to the presidency of the church.[20]

The question became actual rather than theoretical in July 1887, as he learned that the president had died. He felt quite strongly the burden laid upon him, and he called upon the Lord to prepare him "for whatever awaits him on Earth" and to grant him the "power to perform whatever is required at his hands by the God of Heaven." Returning from St. George to Salt Lake

---

[18] Woodruff, *Journal*, 8:344, 350.

[19] Woodruff, *Journal*, 8:421.

[20] Woodruff responded that he himself had "several vary strong reasons why [the apostles discussing the matter] should not." Arguing that with the president's death the apostles became the presiding authority of the church, Woodruff said that the president of the Twelve was effectively the church's president "by virtue of his office as much while presiding over Twelve Apostles as while presiding over two as his Councillors." He said that none of the Twelve had ever claimed to preside over Brigham Young or John Taylor. Furthermore, assuming the conservatism of the church leadership, he thought that because a majority of the Twelve had to agree on the president of the church, it seemed unreasonable to expect them to "depart from the path marked out by inspiration & followed by the Apostles in the death of Christ and also by the Twelve Apostles since the Death of Joseph Smith." He later wrote Grant a letter incorporating the substance of his views. Woodruff, *Journal*, 8:431.

City, on July 29 Woodruff watched Taylor's funeral procession through the same windows he had viewed Phoebe's cortege two years earlier.[21]

The apostles met on August 3 to discuss the governance of the church. They voted to restore George Q. Cannon and Joseph F. Smith to their former positions in the Twelve, but heated opposition to Cannon thwarted Woodruff's desire for an immediate reorganization of the First Presidency. Some of the mud aimed at Cannon splattered on Woodruff, as younger members of the quorum charged they "were men worshipers, sycophants, & [guilty of] todyism."[22]

The Twelve did not resolve the matter or reorganize the First Presidency until the April 1889 conference, in part because of the disputes and in part because George Q. Cannon surrendered himself and spent a term during the fall and winter of 1888–89 in prison.[23]

Although the call of Woodruff, Cannon, and Smith to the First Presidency solved the problem of inaugurating new church leadership, it did not address the more fundamental friction

---

[21] Woodruff, *Journal*, 8:448, 449.

[22] At the August 3, 1887, meeting, several members of the quorum raised the question of Cannon's defense of his son John Q. and the apparent suppression of evidence of the younger Cannon's misdeeds, which included adultery and misappropriation of funds. Succeeding "painful" meetings shortly before the October 1887 and April 1888 conferences led to continued attacks and a division in the council generally between the older members, who supported Cannon, and the younger ones, who opposed him. Woodruff, *Journal*, 8:460. By October 6, 1887, Brigham Young, Jr., thought the quorum had been unified, but subsequent events proved him mistaken. Brigham Young, Jr., Journal, Oct. 6, 1887, Church History Library, Salt Lake City, Utah (hereafter cited as Young Journal). Even though Daniel H. Wells was a counselor to the Twelve rather than a member of the quorum, he was included in the deliberations. Woodruff, *Journal*, 8:489–92. The matter of stock holdings was particularly sticky, because the 60 percent of the stock had been given by John Beck, the founder of the mine, to John Taylor. Generally referred to as the dedicated stock, it was given by Taylor to George Q. Cannon, his nephew, before Taylor's death. Woodruff seems not to have pressed the Twelve to consider reorganizing the Twelve at times other than those proximate to the general conferences, apparently because the general church membership would have to sustain any decision of the Twelve to make it binding.

[23] Woodruff, *Journal*, 8:517, 9:15, 16; Young Journal, Apr. 6, 1888; Journal of Heber J. Grant, Apr. 5, 1889, Church History Library (hereafter cited as Grant Journal).

between American culture and institutions and Mormon doctrines and practices. The most visible of those abrasive issues
was the continued practice of plural marriage and the intense
prosecution it engendered.

As part of the attempt to reduce political opposition to the
church leadership, by 1887 Apostle John W. Young, then living
in New York, had forged extensive links with national Democratic political leaders, through whom he tried to get the federal
government to temporize in its dealings with the Latter-day
Saints. He wrote to President Grover Cleveland's private secretary, Daniel S. Lamont, and to Solicitor General George A.
Jenks, asking that the federal government relieve old and sick
church leaders, particularly Taylor and Woodruff, from the
strain of potential prosecution.[24]

Young's efforts may have succeeded in Woodruff's case. After
Taylor's death, Ireland's successor, Democrat Frank H. Dyer,
told Woodruff that he had not sought to prosecute the aged
leader and that he thought the gentiles should allow those who
had married before the Supreme Court decisions to live out their
lives and that the Mormons should agree not to celebrate any
new plural marriages. Woodruff lived free from fear of prosecution from the fall of 1887 on.[25]

---

[24] John W. Young to Daniel S. Lamont, June 25, 1887, and to George Jenks, July 14, 1887,
John W. Young Letterbooks, 2:71, John W. Young Collection, Beinecke Library, Yale
University (hereafter cited as Young Letterbooks). Shortly after Taylor's death, Young
again renewed the request in behalf of Woodruff, whom he characterized as an eighty-
four-year-old man who had lived away from his home for a long time. Young to "My Dear
Sir" (probably George A. Jenks), July 29, 1887, Young Letterbooks, 2:93. Woodruff was
actually eighty at the time rather than eighty-four.

[25] This discussion is taken from "Report of a private interview held between President Woodruff and United States Marshal Dyer," MS, Oct. 15, 1887, folder 25, Emma Smith Woodruff Collection, Church History Library. In early October 1889, two deputies, apparently
looking for Brigham Young, Jr., stopped Wilford near his farm south of the city. When
he identified himself, they begged his pardon and went on their way. Young Journal,
Oct. 8, 1889. Woodruff told Young that he thought that they wanted him. See also Young
Journal entry for Oct. 12. Dyer may have been unaware of the earlier efforts under his
predecessor to arrest Woodruff.

Dyer's attitude also extended to many other leaders in Salt Lake City, and while federal marshals seemed "more than ordinarily vigilant" in outlying areas north and south, at the center of the church, the leadership sensed "a gradual softening of the feelings of the non-Mormons."[26] By April Conference 1888, most of the Twelve were free to attend.[27]

Moreover, the regime of Democratic appointee and Utah Chief Justice Elliott Sandford promised easier sentences for members of the leadership than under his predecessor, Charles S. Zane. George Q. Cannon and Francis M. Lyman both surrendered voluntarily and entered prison, and the First Presidency suggested selective subjection to the law.[28]

This did not, of course, mean that the federal government would exempt unrepentant polygamists from imprisonment. In fact, in May 1889, 211 cohabs remained incarcerated at Sugarhouse.[29]

---

[26] Wilford Woodruff and George Q. Cannon to John W. Young, Feb. 28, 1888, First Presidency, Letters Sent, Church History Library (hereafter cited as First Presidency Letters). See also Woodruff to William Paxman, Apr. 2, 1888, First Presidency Letters; and Wilford Woodruff to David K. Udall, Oct. 10, 1887, David K. Udall Collection, Church History Library. The intense efforts to apprehend cohabs outside Salt Lake City seem to have resulted from the method by which the federal government paid the deputy U.S. marshals. Instead of giving them a fixed salary as it did Marshal Dyer, the treasury paid the deputies from a portion of the fees collected from the fines levied on those convicted. The anticipation of payment for capture and conviction led to "conspicuous . . . vigilance and zeal" on the part of the deputy marshals north and south of Salt Lake. The cohab hunts in St. George became so intense that Woodruff authorized President McAllister to close the temple if necessary to protect himself and other leading brethren from danger. Wilford Woodruff and George Q. Cannon to John W. Young, Feb. 28, 1888, First Presidency Letters; Young Journal, Apr. 17, 1888; Wilford Woodruff to John D. T. McAllister, Apr. 5, 1888, First Presidency Letters; Wilford Woodruff to William Atkin, Apr. 23, 1888, Wilford Woodruff, Letters to William Atkin Family, 1885–1894, TMs, Utah State Historical Society, Salt Lake City (hereafter cited as Woodruff-Atkin Letters, Utah SHS).

[27] Wilford Woodruff to George Teasdale, Apr. 4, 1888, First Presidency Letters. Brigham Young, Jr., expressed the same sentiment; see Young Journal, Apr. 16 and 17, 1888.

[28] Grant Journal, Sep. 17, Dec. 12, 1888; Franklin D. Richards, Journal, Nov. 21, 1888, Church History Library (hereafter cited as Richards Journal); Young Journal, Dec. 20, 1888; Woodruff, Cannon, and Smith to John D. T. McAllister, May 11, 1889, First Presidency Letters. See also Joseph F. Smith to President Parkinson, Apr. 18, 1889, ibid.

[29] Woodruff, Cannon, and Smith to President Paxman, New Zealand Mission, May 23, 1889, First Presidency Letters.

Beyond the questions of the prosecution of polygamists, other matters seemed pressing. Although the imprisonment of church members caused temporary disruption of normal routine, the church as an institution faced an infinitely more serious challenge. The Morrill Act of 1862 had disincorporated the LDS Church and prohibited any religious organization from owning in excess of $50,000 worth of property in any territory. The 1862 act had carried no enforcement provisions, but the Edmunds-Tucker Act of 1887 established a mechanism for confiscating—or escheating—the church's property for the benefit of the public schools of the territory. The act, however, excluded from escheat buildings and grounds "held and occupied exclusively for purposes of the worship of God, or parsonage connected therewith, or burial grounds."[30] On November 23, 1887, Dyer began to take possession of church properties, which the church rented back, paying the rental fee into the territorial school fund.[31]

---

[30] 22 *U.S. Statutes at Large,* 635 (1887), sec. 13. On Aug. 3, 1887, after discussing Cannon's situation, Woodruff and the Twelve met with attorneys Franklin S. Richards and LeGrand Young about the suit that District Attorney George S. Peters had filed three days earlier to escheat the church property. After some consideration of the matter, in October they agreed to retain James O. Broadhead of St. Louis and former senator Joseph E. McDonald of Indiana to defend the church in the suit. Franklin S. Richards to Wilford Woodruff, Aug. 28, Oct. 7, 1887, Franklin S. Richards Correspondence, Utah SHS (hereafter cited as Richards Correspondence); Grant Journal, July 30, Oct. 6, 1887; Woodruff, *Journal,* 8:462.

[31] The church attorneys entered a demurer, which is a legal proceeding in which a defendant does not dispute the allegations of the prosecution but denies that they are sufficient to justify legal action. The court declined to sustain the demurer. On the appointment of the receiver, see F S Richards to Wilford Woodruff, Nov. 9, 1887, Richards Correspondence; Wilford Woodruff to John Henry Smith, Nov. 14, 1887, John Henry Smith Papers in the George Albert Smith Family Papers, box 11, folder 28, Western Americana, Marriott Library, University of Utah (hereafter cited as Smith Papers). In sum, the suit asked recovery of $3 million in church property. Woodruff rightly thought they would not get "that much." Woodruff, *Journal,* 8:456. The church rented the properties back, paying $12 per year for the temple block, $2,400 for the tithing office, and $1,200 for the Gardo House. Lewis Allen (Woodruff) to William Atkin, Nov. 24, 1887, Woodruff-Atkin Letters, Utah SHS; John M. Whitaker Daily Journal, part 5, p. 11, Typescript, Mormon File, Huntington Library, San Marino, California. For a comprehensive discussion of the escheated property and its value, see Leonard J. Arrington, *Great Basin Kingdom: An Economic History of the Latter-day Saints, 1890–1930* (Cambridge, Mass.: Harvard University Press, 1958), 360–73.

In 1887, the church leadership sought to finesse the confiscation proceedings by applying for the admission of Utah as a state. Had they succeeded, they would have freed themselves from the provisions of the Morrill, Edmunds, and Edmunds-Tucker Acts, because the laws applied only in territories and not in states. This was the sixth time that Utah had tried to obtain statehood, each of the efforts coming at a critical juncture.[32]

Woodruff and the church leadership sent several representatives to Washington to lobby for statehood.[33] In Washington, the lobbyists enlisted the aid of Democratic representative William L. Scott of Pennsylvania and prominent political insider Judge George Ticknor Curtis. In February 1888, Wilford Woodruff sent Joseph F. Smith to Washington as leader of the lobbying effort to replace John W. Young, in whom they had lost confidence.[34]

The lobbyists tried first to attach an amendment, proposed by Representative Scott, to the Edmunds-Tucker Act. The amendment would have placed a six-month moratorium on the enforcement of the law to allow the Utahns to adopt a constitution with a provision prohibiting polygamy.[35] Strong opposition

[32] For a brief discussion of each of these attempts, see E. Leo Lyman, *Political Deliverance: The Mormon Quest for Utah Statehood* (Urbana: University of Illinois Press, 1986), chapter 1. For a more thorough discussion, see Jerome Bernstein, "A History of the Constitutional Conventions of the Territory of Utah from 1849–1895," master's thesis, Utah State University, 1961. The other conventions had been held in 1849, following settlement; 1856, during the reformation; 1861, as the new Republican administration prepared to take power; 1872, during Judge James B. McKean's judicial crusade; and 1882, following the passage of the Edmunds Act.

[33] Those sent included Apostle John W. Young, who led the group, Franklin S. Richards, Charles W. Penrose, William W. Riter, Brother Woolley (probably Samuel E. Woolley or Edwin G. Woolley), and Utah delegate John T. Caine.

[34] Wilford Woodruff to "Whom it May Concern," Feb. 10, 1888, to Franklin S. Richards and Charles W. Penrose, Apr. 11, 1888, First Presidency Letters; idem to Joseph F. Smith, Apr. 25, 1888, First Presidency Letters; Woodruff and Cannon to Joseph F. Smith, Apr. 5, 1888, Woodruff Letterbooks, Church History Library; Grant Journal, May 19, 1888.

[35] See Lyman, *Political Deliverance,* 42; George Ticknor Curtis to George Q. Cannon, Jan. 25, 1887, and John W. Young telegram to First Presidency, Feb. 2, 1887, in First Presidency Minutes, 1887, Church History Library.

from House Judiciary Committee chairman and bill sponsor
J. Randolph Tucker of Virginia thwarted the Pennsylvania congressman's efforts, and the bill passed quickly.

The constitutional convention met in Salt Lake City from
June 30 through July 7, 1887. Thereafter, the Utah lobbyists tried
to get the Cleveland administration and members of Congress
to accept their good faith in voting to prohibit polygamy in the
constitution. Cleveland and many other Democrats seemed
convinced of the church's sincerity, but several powerful Republican leaders in the Senate were not.[36]

The efforts to achieve statehood revealed the status of Woodruff's odyssey and the degree to which the church leadership had
changed its views and was prepared to compromise by late 1887
and early 1888. The Senate Committee on Territories conducted
hearings on the Utah Constitution in February and March
1888. Senator McDonald, Judge Wilson, and attorney Richards
presented the case. Richards, Joseph F. Smith, and Charles W.
Penrose coached the other two before the hearings, and Penrose
formulated various arguments focusing on church doctrine and
practice. Using a textual argument, Richards interpreted the
words of Joseph Smith's revelation on plural marriage to mean
that the church considered the practice permissive rather than
mandatory for its members. He admitted that individuals might
interpret the words as commanding the practice of polygamy
but insisted that the revelation itself did not warrant such an
interpretation. Furthermore, Richards indicated the church's
willingness to conform to the requirements and demands of the
law, which was passed to punish actual offenders.

In arguing the case against priesthood domination in political and economic matters, Richards focused on the allegation

---

[36] See Grant Journal, Nov. 14, 1887; Franklin S. Richards to Wilford Woodruff, George Q.
Cannon, and Joseph F. Smith, Dec. 17, 1887, Richards Correspondence; Lyman, *Political
Deliverance*, 57.

that tithing constituted a tax on church members exacted under priesthood sanctions. He said that members paid tithing as a voluntary contribution and not a church tax. From this example, he deduced the freedom of the members to follow or ignore the advice of church leaders.[37] Reading press reports and letters from Richards and others, Woodruff felt encouraged by the efforts, but Congress did not act.[38]

In early 1889, Wilford Woodruff recognized that "statehood, to all outward appearance, is shelved for an indefinite period."[39] He knew that in the absence of statehood, Utah remained, "politically speaking, a dependency or ward of the United States." Moreover, statehood promised deliverance from what he perceived as a future rather than an imminent apocalypse, because "in the event of the disruption of the general government [we would] be independent of all earthly powers and clothed with legal as well as divine authority to assume the position in the earth God has designed or may design us to fill."[40]

---

[37] Richards to Wilford Woodruff and George Q. Cannon, Feb. 28, Mar. 22, 1888, Richards Correspondence. In August 1887, Richards had made similar points in a letter to George Ticknor Curtis. He pointed out that when the revelation was first received, many entered the practice because they believed the revelation made the practice mandatory. Many who did not enter did so on the plea that it was permissive, not mandatory. The difference of opinion as to the construction still exists. Still, he pointed out, the people were united in believing that the prohibitory clauses of the 1887 constitution ought to be enforced. Richards to George Ticknor Curtis, Aug. 27, 1887, ibid. At a later hearing, Richards attacked the harsh methods used in the arrest and conviction of polygamists in Utah.

[38] Wilford Woodruff to William M. Paxman, Apr. 2, and to George Teasdale, Apr. 4, 1888, First Presidency Letters. In November 1888, the Presidency and Twelve agreed to send Penrose and Richards back to Washington for a renewed effort to secure statehood during the lame duck session of Congress. Grant Journal, Nov. 13, 1888. By then, however, political conditions had changed. Harrison had defeated Cleveland in the presidential election, and the public had returned a solidly Republican Congress. Recognizing the animosity against the Mormons, the Democratic Congress and president ignored Utah and voted to admit the Dakotas, Montana, and Washington instead. Lyman, *Political Deliverance*, 107.

[39] Woodruff to George Teasdale, Feb. 12, 1889, First Presidency Letters.

[40] Lewis Allen (Woodruff) to William Atkin, Jan. 30, 1889, Woodruff-Atkin Letters, Utah SHS.

Given the critical need for support to achieve statehood, Wilford Woodruff and the church leadership pressed the church officials and press to soft-pedal their rhetoric. They tried to suppress antigovernment commentary in the church-controlled press, counseled missionaries to remain low-key in their proselyting efforts, and reproved general authorities who publicly supported or encouraged plural marriage.[41]

Even after it became abundantly clear in early 1889 that Congress and the president would never approve Utah's 1887 constitution, the Presidency and Twelve pressed to restrain the actions and statements encouraging polygamy. On March 13, 1889, the

---

[41] In November 1887, the leadership came down rather hard on the publishers of the Salt Lake *Herald*, advising them to exercise caution in criticizing the federal government. Wilford Woodruff, George Q. Cannon, and Joseph F. Smith to Charles W. Penrose, Nov. 22, 1887, Wilford Woodruff Letters, Church History Library (hereafter cited as Woodruff Letters). In 1887 and 1888, criticism arose among Democratic supporters of the church in Congress over the intense proselyting efforts of Mormon missionaries in the South. Complaints from southern Evangelical ministers and other constituents of the congressmen and senators made the lawmakers wary of supporting the Mormon cause. As a result, Woodruff counseled Southern States Mission President William Spry to caution his missionaries about "raising excitement upon our question and stirring up feeling among their constituents." The church president urged missionaries to continue to preach but "to pursue a conciliatory policy and to do everything in [their] power to allay prejudice and to quiet down hostility." Wilford Woodruff and George Q. Cannon to Joseph F. Smith, Apr. 5, 1888, and Wilford Woodruff to William Spry, June 15, 1888, Woodruff Letters. In the April 1888 General Conference, Seymour B. Young and Rudger Clawson "branched off onto Polygamy," and the lobbyists in the east telegraphed that their "remarks have done much damage to the cause of statehood." Young Journal, Apr. 7, 1888. In May 1888, Joseph F. Smith wrote that "the arrest and conviction of a single 'polygamist' would do more, towards nullifying all that has been done, and towards blocking the way for statehood, than anything, short of an open avowal of a continuance [of the practice of plural marriage] by the Authorities of the Church." Smith said that he did not intend "to compromise with the Devil, or relinquish one iota of revealed truth, nor a wife or child, [but that] it seems wisdom to halt, and plan, and maneuver to defeat the full purpose of the foe, and to prevent suffering, persecutions, and the many horrors of legalized mobocracy." Joseph F. Smith to John Henry Smith, May 9, 1888, Smith Papers, box 11, folder 22. Moses Thatcher's defiant attitude upon his arrest in September 1888 and a talk by John Nicholson in the October 1888 General Conference also led to censure by the church leadership in view "of the policy decided upon" by the First Presidency and Twelve. Wilford Woodruff to Charles O. Card, Sep. 6, 1888, First Presidency Letters; Grant Journal, Oct. 7, 1888.

First Presidency and Twelve met in a council at the Gardo House, with John W. Taylor. Taylor had publicly attacked as a "damned lie" Utah delegate John T. Caine's declaration that polygamy was a dead issue in Utah. Duly reported in the *Salt Lake Tribune*, Taylor's outburst created an immediate stir. Confronted by President Woodruff, Elder Taylor "manifested a vary Bad spirit." He said that anyone who said polygamy was not mandatory was "a liar and the truth is not in him." He made many other accusations as well but eventually agreed to make "any reparation necessary."[42]

This does not mean that plural marriages ceased. Rather, those who solemnized them performed the marriages quietly, out of the public eye, and preferably in Mexico.[43]

After Phoebe's death, Wilford arranged his family affairs to abide by a strict interpretation of the Edmunds Act. He became a practicing monogamist but a spiritual polygamist. During the early 1880s, he had spent little time with Delight, who lived near Emma's farm south of Salt Lake City. Sarah and their son Newton lived in Smithfield, and he had often visited there. In February 1884, as Woodruff visited in Logan for the temple dedication, he stayed at the home he and Sarah shared in Smithfield.[44] On August 3, 1890, he visited Sarah's house in Smithfield, the first time he had done so "for seven years."[45]

---

[42] Woodruff, *Journal*, 9:13; Richards Journal, Mar. 13, 1889; Grant Journal, Mar. 13, 1889. Those present were Wilford Woodruff, George Q. Cannon, Joseph F. Smith, Franklin D. Richards, John Henry Smith, Moses Thatcher, and Heber J. Grant.

[43] In at least one case in May 1888, Woodruff authorized A. F. MacDonald to perform a plural marriage for Ammon Tenney in Mexico. Wilford Woodruff to A. F. McDonald, May 3, 1888, First Presidency Letters. The authorities urged those who had recently entered plural marriage to remain quiet about the practice. In October 1889, Abraham H. Cannon urged a Brother Jorgason of Sevier County to keep the date of a sealing to his plural wife secret because it had occurred during the previous three years. Abraham H. Cannon Journal, Oct. 21, 1889, L. Tom Perry Special Collections, Harold B. Lee Library, Brigham Young University, Provo, Utah (hereafter cited as Cannon Journal).

[44] Woodruff, *Journal*, 8:227.

[45] Woodruff, *Journal*, 9:103.

When not on the underground, however, he had spent most of his time either with Phoebe or with Emma. After Phoebe's death, Woodruff appeared publicly only with Emma, though he entertained his other families and children at private celebrations such as his birthday.[46]

Moreover, he began to spend his private time with the children Emma had borne him rather than with his other families. Although he corresponded with his other wives and children, his diary from the mid-1880s through 1890 is full of visits, work, and vacations with Asahel, Abraham Owen, and Clara and her husband, Ovando Beebe. He seldom met with his other children except on family business. He corresponded with many of his children, but most often with Phoebe's and Emma's, and with Newton, who seems to have taken his father's place in caring for and repairing Sarah's home in Smithfield. Moreover, although Wilford corresponded with Sarah and Delight, he seldom wrote to any of the children Delight had borne him and to any of Sarah's children except Newton.[47]

As the March 1889 inauguration of Benjamin Harrison neared, the church leadership feared the renewal of intense prosecution from the generally hostile Republicans. Even though Cleveland remained in office between the election and inauguration, relations seemed tense and Woodruff thought—erroneously, as it proved—that the new Democratic attorney general for Utah, George Peters, might want to demonstrate his vigilance by having the grand jury indict Cannon, Smith, and others for adultery.[48]

The president and representatives of the new Republican administration promised to temporize, but in practice their

---

[46] Woodruff, *Journal*, 8:232. In 1885, he was hiding out in Bunkerville, Nevada. Ibid., 8:306.

[47] This generalization is based on a cursory examination of Woodruff's diary entries for the period 1886 through 1890. He generally wrote in his diary the names of the people with whom he carried on a private correspondence. He carried on a correspondence with one of his daughters named Phoebe, but this seems to have been Phoebe Amelia, Phoebe's child, rather than Phoebe Arabella, whom Sarah bore him.

[48] Woodruff to George Teasdale, Feb. 12, 1889, First Presidency Letters.

regime became more harsh.[49] In Idaho, for instance, the legis-lature banned Mormons from voting, and at admission in 1890 the state enshrined the principle in constitutional law.[50]

In Utah, the federal government broadened its attack on the Latter-day Saints in late 1889 by refusing to naturalize Mormon immigrants. On November 14, 1889, Judge Thomas J. Anderson, sitting temporarily as third district judge, began hearings in Salt Lake City on the petition of John Moore, a Mormon immigrant from Great Britain. At the time, an intense political contest for control of the Salt Lake City government had ensued, and Joseph Lipman of the *Salt Lake Tribune*, representing the Lib-eral Party, had hired former U.S. attorney William H. Dickson and former assistant U.S. attorney Robert N. Baskin to oppose Moore's petition. They charged the Mormons with disloyalty to the United States government.[51]

The court concerned itself with the loyalty of members of the church to the United States government and collective disdain for the law rather than personal sexual habits. In the hearing, several Mormon excommunicants testified that they had taken vows against the government because of the murder of Joseph and Hyrum Smith. The prosecution also read passages on such

---

[49] Shortly after the inauguration, Jeremiah M. Wilson, on retainer as church attorney in Washington, met with Attorney General William H. H. Miller, and Franklin S. Rich-ards visited with Harrison and with Secretary of State James G. Blaine. Both church representatives urged the appointment of conservative men of high character who would enforce the law evenhandedly. Both Miller and Harrison said they expected no appoint-ments of vindictive or unfriendly officials, and Blaine told Richards that he thought the government should not try to stamp out individual belief through persecution and that the officers should enforce the laws justly. Franklin S. Richards to Wilford Woodruff, George Q. Cannon, and Joseph F. Smith, Apr. 13, 1889, Richards Correspondence, Utah SHS; Wilford Woodruff, George Q. Cannon, and Joseph F. Smith to Jeremiah M. Wil-son, May 25, 1889, First Presidency Letters.

[50] Grant Journal, July 31, 1890. Wyoming kept a similar prohibition out of its 1890 constitu-tion largely because of lobbying among members of the Republican Party, which church members agreed to support.

[51] For a summary of the events associated with the naturalization and endowment oath case, see James R. Clark, ed. *Messages of the First Presidency of the Church of Jesus Christ of Lat-ter-day Saints, 1833–1964* (Salt Lake City: Bookcraft, 1966), 3:171–74.

subjects as blood atonement from the *Journal of Discourses* and the *Millennial Star* to support their contention that Mormons were disloyal.[52]

Because Woodruff, Cannon, and Smith were away visiting Saints in Canada, the Twelve devised means of defense until their return on November 16, selecting various apostles and prominent lay members to testify.[53] In addition to active church members, the church called Elias L. T. Harrison, who had been a leader in the dissident Godbeite movement, and several other non-Mormons who had received endowments. They all testified that Mormons took no oath against the government.[54]

In rebuttal, Dickson put Henry W. Lawrence, another prominent Godbeite, on the stand. Lawrence testified that he had officiated in the Endowment House from 1865 through 1869 and had administered oaths "inimical to the interests of the government."[55]

Although Wilford Woodruff did not appear in court, he gave an interview to an Associated Press reporter on the case. Woodruff said that the members of the church staunchly supported the U.S. Constitution and the government. Although

---

[52] Cannon Journal, Nov. 14, 15, 1889.

[53] Cannon Journal, Nov. 11, 12, 13, 1889; Grant Journal, Nov. 12, 1889. Some of the Twelve misperceived the issue, thinking that "adultery and illicit intercourse" might bar those applying for citizenship. They thought the court inconsistent in admitting to citizenship without question gentiles who engaged in such practices while proposing to deny the privilege to Mormons because of their belief in polygamy.

[54] Cannon Journal, Nov. 16, 18, 1889; Young Journal, Nov. 17, 1889; Grant Journal, Nov. 17, 1889.

[55] Cannon Journal, Nov. 20, 21, 1889. After the hearings, during a meeting held to determine a course of action to be taken, Cannon said, "In speaking of the recent examination before Judge Anderson . . . that he understood when he had his endowments in Nauvoo that he took an oath against the murderers of the Prophet Joseph as well as other prophets, and if he had ever met any of those who had taken a hand in that massacre he would undoubtedly have attempted to avenge the blood of the martyrs." Ibid., Dec. 6, 1889. After appearing, Charles W. Penrose spent a day in prison for contempt for refusing to answer Dickson's query about how many wives he had. George Q. Cannon also appeared under subpoena, but the questions asked of him bore only on the attempts of the church to defend its rights and not on the question of an endowment oath.

admitting the secrecy of the endowment ceremony, he said the ritual contained nothing threatening or treasonable. Counterattacking, he also charged that the Liberals had pressed the suit for political purposes.[56]

Apparently recognizing the contradictory testimony on the endowment oath, Judge Anderson nevertheless issued a sweeping indictment of church doctrine and practice. Anderson based his ruling on public statements of church leaders, particularly their emphasis on millennialism and the imminence of the apocalypse. Beginning with the premise that the church taught that their organization was the actual Kingdom of God on earth with authority vested in the priesthood, Anderson ruled that it perceived itself as a temporal and spiritual kingdom holding the authority to control all aspects of the lives of its members. He cited the church's millennial doctrines that the Kingdom of God would eventually overthrow the United States and all other governments and showed that church leaders had preached blood atonement for certain sins. He pointed out also that the church believed that polygamy was a commandment of God and cited statements of general authorities taking issue with the Reynolds decision and insisting that all laws interfering with religion were unconstitutional.[57]

The naturalization case became the catalyst for a new revelation and several other church initiatives. On Sunday, November 24, Woodruff met at the Gardo House with the lawyers handling the case. They urged him to make some concession to the court on polygamy and other questions. After hearing their pleas, Woodruff retired from the group and spent several hours alone enquiring of the Lord about the matter. Following his inquiry, he received a revelation on the subject.

---

[56] Journal History, Church History Library, Nov. 22, 23, 1889.
[57] Cannon Journal, Nov. 30, 1889.

The revelation reaffirmed the basic principles that the church leadership had taught previously, but in a much less strident or apocalyptic tone than the 1880 wilderness revelation. The church leadership was told not to "deny my word or my law." The revelation said they should not place "yourselves in jeopardy to your enemies by promise." The document instructed the lawyers to "make their pleadings as they are moved upon by the Holy spirit, without any further pledges from the Priesthood." The Lord promised he would "hold the courts, with the officers of government, and the nation responsible for their acts towards the inhabitants of Zion." The revelation promised further that the Lord would remain with the Saints and that he would pour out His judgments "upon all nations under the heavens which include great Babylon." The judgments stood "at the door," and the Lord promised to deliver the Saints from the wicked "in mine own due time and way."[58]

By the early part of December 1889, Woodruff and his counselors had come to feel quite deeply the burdens they and the church bore. By that time, the Utah Territorial Supreme Court had issued its decision sustaining the escheat of church property, and while the church had appealed the case to the U.S. Supreme Court, the higher court had not yet rendered its decision.

President Woodruff's attitudes had changed considerably by that time. Instead of taking a defiant attitude as in 1880 and calling upon the Lord to curse the leaders of the nation, he instead worked with his counselors to draft a circular letter to presidents of stakes to pray that the Lord would soften the hearts of the executive, cabinet, Senate, House of Representatives, judiciary, and people of the nation toward the people of God. They urged members of the church to spend Joseph Smith's birthday

---

[58] Woodruff, *Journal*, 9:67–69. Apparently, the revelation was well received by members of the Twelve. See Young Journal, Nov. 24, 1889; Cannon Journal, Dec. 19, 1889.

(December 23, 1889) in fasting and prayer, calling upon the Lord to "interfere in behalf of his people and preserve them from the power of their enemies and incline the hearts of the rulers of the nation to us." They urged members to pray "for a righteous decision in the Church suits now pending before the" Supreme Court.[59]

The circular letter labeled an "Official Declaration," generally called "the Manifesto of the Apostles," was drafted by Charles W. Penrose. Edited and signed by the First Presidency and Twelve on December 12,[60] the declaration began by setting the events in the context of the recent naturalization hearings. It denied that the church preached blood atonement, said that church courts had no right to "supersede, annul or modify a judgment of any civil court," and asserted that the church did "not claim or exercise the right to interfere with citizens in the free exercise of social or political rights and privileges." Furthermore, it said, nothing in the endowment ceremony or in any doctrine of the church was "hostile to the Government of the United States." The declaration also said that although the Latter-day Saints proclaimed that "the kingdom of heaven is

---

[59] Clark, *Messages of the First Presidency,* 3:176–79. President Woodruff had given the interview to the Associated Press and had received the revelation of November 24 nearly a week before Judge Anderson had issued his ruling, and the circular letter of December 12 had been issued before the Presidency and Twelve had considered a proper response to the ruling. On December 6, however, Woodruff met with the First Presidency, the Twelve, and the People's Party Central Committee to agree on a course of action to counter the bad publicity engendered by Anderson's decision. Those present concurred in a threefold set of tactics. First, the First Presidency and apostles agreed to prepare and sign "a dignified paper, without even mentioning the actions of the Courts, setting forth our doctrines, and denying the . . . charges of our murderous character and disloyalty to the government." Second, local Mormon businessmen planned to issue a paper "giving the lie to Anderson's statements." Following these two announcements, members were to hold mass meetings throughout the territory to protest the robbery of the franchise. Cannon Journal, Dec. 6, 1889; Grant Journal, Dec. 6, 1889.

[60] Cannon Journal, Dec. 12, 1889; Grant Journal, Dec. 28, 1889. The First Presidency telegraphed those apostles who were available for permission to attach their signatures, and Woodruff authorized the signatures of those whom they could not reach.

at hand," the church did not constitute itself an *"imperium in imperio"* aimed at overthrowing the United States or any other civil government.[61]

Although prospects seemed particularly bleak by early 1890 and the promises of Harrison administration officials to administer the law evenhandedly seemed to fly in the face of Judge Anderson's ruling and the continued efforts to confiscate church property, conditions were already beginning to change. Shortly after John Taylor's death in 1887, George Q. Cannon and Joseph F. Smith worked through Hiram B. Clawson to contact a group of California Republican leaders. After Woodruff returned to Salt Lake City, he began operating directly with the group.

The political initiatives taken with the Californians sought to neutralize Republican opposition and to ally certain prominent GOP leaders with the Latter-day Saint effort for justice and eventual statehood.

On September 15, 1887, Wilford Woodruff met personally with Alexander Badlam and Isaac Trumbo of San Francisco. Badlam, a California businessman, was a nephew of Samuel Brannan. More important, he had been president of the Boston Branch of the church while Woodruff was president of the Eastern States Mission from 1848 through 1850. During the late 1840s, Woodruff and Badlam had become good friends. Woodruff had encouraged Badlam to emigrate to California to prospect for gold, and upon his return, Alexander had given Wilford a present of nine and a half ounces of the yellow metal.[62]

After the initial meeting in September 1887, Woodruff, Cannon, and their associates met and corresponded with Badlam

[61] Clark, *Messages of the First Presidency*, 3:184–87. Early in 1890, the First Presidency and Twelve took other measures to deal with these problems. On January 1, Woodruff, Smith, and Grant set apart L. John Nuttall to go to Washington to work with delegate John T. Caine; and they called John Morgan and B. H. Roberts of the First Council of the Seventy to speak in the interest of the people against the prejudice "engendered by the late decision of Judge Anderson." Grant Journal, Jan. 1, 1890.
[62] See Woodruff, *Journal*, 3:385, 412, 420–22, 435, 477, 537, 538.

and Trumbo on other occasions.[63] Between Woodruff's first meeting with the two in September 1887 and the end of 1888, the two held interviews with Woodruff and other church leaders, supplying information including data on conditions in the East.[64] During March and April as Joseph F. Smith and other leaders worked with Democrats in the East for statehood, Badlam worked to influence leading Republican newspapers of the country on behalf of the statehood effort.[65]

After church officials became convinced that the Democratic Party could not deliver statehood for Utah, Woodruff and Cannon took more direct measures to deal with the Republicans. In April 1889 after Harrison's inauguration, and less than a week after Woodruff's call as president of the church, Wilford and several other prominent Mormons took a twelve-day trip to California to visit Badlam, Trumbo, and other political and business leaders. They met twice with Senator Leland Stanford, whom Woodruff called "a true friend of ours," and once with others from the Southern Pacific crowd, including Collis P. Huntington,

---

[63] Isaac Trumbo, a former Utah resident, was a second cousin of Hiram B. Clawson's and a major stockholder in the Bullion, Beck, and Champion Mining Company. Working through Clawson, also a Bullion, Beck stockholder, in July 1887 the two Californians had already offered Cannon and Smith their services and the connections with Leland Stanford and other Southern Pacific Railroad Company officials in Utah's efforts to achieve statehood. On July 27, 1887, shortly after John Taylor's death, Cannon and Smith had sent a letter of introduction to Leland Stanford in Clawson's behalf, but until Woodruff opened the direct discussions with Badlam and Trumbo, the church leaders had apparently worked through Clawson rather than dealing with the California group directly. George Q. Cannon and Joseph F. Smith to Leland Stanford, July 27, 1887, First Presidency Letters; see Lyman, *Political Deliverance,* 73–78, 93n. The only contact with the California group seems to have been a letter of introduction given to Clawson and addressed to Leland Stanford by Cannon and Smith in July 1887. The extent of the contact with Cannon and Smith before this time will probably not be known until the George Q. Cannon diaries are made available. Trumbo was also interested in other affairs, such as the promotion of a railroad from Salt Lake City to Los Angeles. Woodruff, *Journal,* 8:459.

[64] Woodruff, *Journal,* 8:470, 484, 486, 493, 504, 505, 506, 516.

[65] Woodruff and Cannon to Joseph F. Smith, Mar. 13, Apr. 5, 1888, Woodruff Letters. Heber J. Grant did not share the enthusiasm for Badlam that Woodruff, Cannon, and Smith did, saying that he did not "have any confidence in [Badlam] or his company," the Bankers and Merchants Mutual Life Insurance Company of California. Grant Journal, July 3, 1888.

a director and later president of the line; A. N. Towne, general superintendent; and Stephen T. Gage, an SP lobbyist.[66] Stanford said he thought Harrison was bigoted, but the senator said he was willing "to do everything in his power for [the Mormons'] good," including writing Harrison on their behalf. They also met with Judge Morris M. Estee, who had presided at the Republican Convention that nominated Harrison. Woodruff said, "[Estee] feels very kindly disposed, and desirous to do us good."[67]

In addition to opening contacts with Democratic leaders through the lobbying efforts in the East and personal contact through Republican politicians in California, the church leadership began to loosen its hold on politics in Salt Lake City, in part from necessity, in part from conviction. Several of the Twelve—particularly Heber J. Grant—believed that the church had remained far too closed in its political relationships with others. As early as December 1887, Grant wrote that the church ought to be more "liberal before we are forced to be for considerations of policy." He went on to observe that he was "as much opposed to aiding and supporting our enemies as it is possible for a man to be" but was "willing to grant them representation in our City, County and Territorial government where they are good and substantial citizens."[68] On December 29, the First Presidency, Heber J. Grant and John W. Taylor of the Twelve, and several local People's Party leaders, including Mayor Francis Armstrong and members of the city council, met at Woodruff's office. They discussed the advisability of inviting Liberal Party members to run for the Salt Lake city council on a joint ticket. The group approved the proposal, some arguing that it was good policy under the circumstances,

[66] Woodruff wrote in his journal that the individual was named Mr. Gay, but the person in question was probably Gage, since he worked as a lobbyist for the Southern Pacific group. See Stuart Daggett, *Chapters on the History of the Southern Pacific* (New York: Ronald Press, 1922), 209–10.
[67] Woodruff, *Journal*, 9:17–27.
[68] Grant Journal, Dec. 29, 1888.

and others like Grant favoring it "because they thought it just."[69] In the February 1888 election, however, the coalition slate, styled the Citizen's Ticket, won quite handily.[70]

Following the victory of the Citizen's Ticket in Salt Lake City in February 1888, many Latter-day Saints favored the breakup of the People's Party and perhaps even its merger with the Utah Territorial Democratic Party. Woodruff and the church leadership opposed the proposal.[71]

Nevertheless, although Woodruff and the church leadership opposed the merger and worked to open the Republican Party, they supported the national Democratic Party in the 1888 election. They provided money to help subvent the publication of newspapers, provided funds for Cleveland's presidential campaign, supported Democratic candidates in other states, and sent Franklin S. Richards and Joseph F. Smith as observers to the Democratic convention in St. Louis. Alexander Badlam and Isaac Trumbo tried to keep Republican Party newspapers in line in an effort directed by the First Presidency rather than through the larger church political apparatus, perhaps because

[69] Grant Journal, Dec. 29, 1887; Woodruff, *Journal*, 8:473–74.

[70] Woodruff, *Journal*, 8:482; B. H. Roberts, *Comprehensive History of the Church of Jesus Christ of Latter-day Saints, Century I*, 6 vols. (Salt Lake City: Deseret News Press, 1930), 6:201. A committee made up of William W. Riter, John Clark, and Samuel P. Teasdel left the meeting to contact Liberal Party leaders. After discussing the matter with Governor Caleb West, Marshal Frank H. Dyer, Joseph L. Rawlins, U.S. Attorney William H. Dickson, J. R. McBride, and others, they agreed to nominate four prominent businessmen: W. S. McCornick, John E. Dooley, M. B. Sowles, and Boliver Roberts. The church leadership also considered having the legislature redistrict the city so certain areas with a predominance of gentiles would elect Liberal representatives, but the 1888 legislature met too late to effect the change for that year.

[71] See Lyman, *Political Deliverance*, 100–103; Richards Journal, May 7, 1888; Grant Journal, Oct. 22, 1888. Three attorneys from Provo—Samuel R. Thurman, Warren Dusenberry, and William H. King—led a Mormon contingent to the Democratic Party convention in Ogden in April 1888. The convention expelled the Mormons, but about one hundred of them had held a competing Democratic Party convention, nominated Thurman for Congress, and sought recognition from the national party. In succeeding months, the national party rebuffed them, Woodruff and the church leaders opposed their efforts, and John T. Caine, the People's Party candidate, soundly defeated both Thurman and the Liberal Party candidate.

the leadership recognized the hatred most Mormons bore toward the Republican Party.[72]

In a very real sense, events in 1889 marked the beginning of the end for Mormon political domination of the Utah political scene. The Edmunds Act in 1882 had disfranchised all practicing polygamists, and the 1887 Edmunds-Tucker Act added insult to injury by disfranchising all Utah women, an overwhelming majority of whom were Mormons. The general economic prosperity of the late 1880s, coupled with a mining boom that affected Utah business in particular, swelled the ranks of gentile voters. Judge Anderson's ruling in the Moore case meant that no further Mormon immigrants would be admitted to citizenship, and the activities of the Utah Commission and its registration agents further reduced the ranks of Mormon voters.

Under the circumstances, the tentative efforts to begin to open the political process, coupled with continued control over party machinery evidenced by the 1888 Citizen's Ticket and the support for Cleveland in 1888, proved too little too late. A major crack in the dike that earlier Mormon leaders had built to separate themselves from Babylon came in the fall 1888 elections as several Liberal Party candidates won election to the territorial legislature. Hard on the heels of this loss, the church suffered a larger defeat in the Ogden, Utah, municipal election of February 1889 as the Liberal Party captured control of the city government.

In view of the previous events, the February 1890 municipal elections in Salt Lake City became a battleground on which Woodruff and the church leadership staked their political

---

[72] Jason Mack (Joseph F. Smith) to James Jack, Mar. 20, 1888, Jason Mack Papers, Church History Library; Wilford Woodruff and George Q. Cannon to John T. Caine, May 9, 1888, Woodruff Letterbooks, Church History Library; idem to Joseph F. Smith, May 11, 1888, ibid.; James Jack to John T. Caine, May 12, 25, 1888, ibid.; Wilford Woodruff to Joseph F. Smith, Charles W. Penrose, and Franklin S. Richards, May 22, 1888, First Presidency Letters; Grant Journal, Oct. 15, 16, 20, 24, 1888.

future.[73] In anticipation of the election, LDS officials had the city accelerate its public works program to bring in more workmen who would vote the People's Party ticket. Members of the church leadership also worked with members to try to get them to take the Edmunds-Tucker oath in order to vote, though some refused to do so on the ground that such action would be immoral. Some authorities suggested a fusion ticket similar to that offered in 1888, but most doubted that gentiles would agree, because by late January the Liberal Party had two thousand more names on the voter registration lists than the People's Party. In addition, the Liberal Party, which controlled the registration lists, had purged a large number of Mormon names.

The whole situation is difficult to sort out, but the Liberal Party majority resulted from several initiatives. The large number of Liberal voters resulted, in part, from agents registering nonresident voters along the Denver and Rio Grande railroad line between Salt Lake and Pleasant Valley Junction. Registration officials began to strike the names of legitimate People's Party voters on allegations of polygamy, nonresidence, and alien status.[74]

---

[73] The following information on the 1890 election in Salt Lake City is based on Cannon Journal, Oct. 11, 17, 18, 19, Nov. 12, Dec. 28, 1889, Jan. 8, 14, 20, 23, 27, 29, 31, Feb. 3, 6, 7, 9, 1890; Wilford Woodruff to George Q. Cannon, Feb. 3, 1890, First Presidency Letters; Wilford Woodruff and Joseph F. Smith to George Q. Cannon, Jan. 21, 1890, ibid.; Wilford Woodruff (per James Jack) and Joseph F. Smith to Moses Thatcher, Jan. 23, 1890, ibid.; Wilford Woodruff and Joseph F. Smith to George Teasdale, Jan. 27, 1890, ibid.; First Presidency to George Q. Cannon, Jan. 29, 1890, ibid.; Wilford Woodruff to Abraham O. Smoot, Jan. 30, 1890, ibid.; Wilford Woodruff and Joseph F. Smith to George Q. Cannon, Jan. 29, 1890, Woodruff Letterbooks, Church History Library; James Jack to John T. Caine, Jan. 29, 1890, ibid.; Wilford Woodruff to George Q. Cannon, Feb. 3, 1890, ibid.; Grant Journal, Jan. 8, 9, 20, 21, 23, 25, 29, Feb. 3, 5, 8, 10, 1890.

[74] To counter the fraudulent voting lists, the First Presidency sent Heber J. Grant and John Clark to Denver to meet with David C. Dodge of the Denver and Rio Grande Railroad. Dodge ordered the local railroad officials, particularly W. H. Bancroft (superintendent of the Utah Division in Salt Lake) not to meddle in politics, and he opened the railroad's payroll records so that church officials could search for registered nonresidents employed by the railroad. For a history of the Denver and Rio Grande Western, see Robert G. Athearn, *Rebel of the Rockies: A History of the Denver and Rio Grande Western Railroad* (New Haven, Conn.: Yale University Press, 1962).

As the election returns began to come in, it became evident that the People's Party had lost by a sizeable majority. Mayoral candidate and Salt Lake City businessman George M. Scott defeated Spencer Clawson by 808 votes.[75] On reflection, church officials recognized that they could do little because the grand jury, which would have to return indictments, was firmly controlled by the gentiles.[76] Adding insult to injury, the mayor refused to seat three winning People's Party candidates for the city council despite their certification by Judge Zane.[77]

Both in public and in private, Wilford Woodruff proclaimed that the Liberals had stolen the city election. In an interview given to the Associated Press, he said that he considered "the election has been gained here by striking from the registration lists hundreds of legally qualified citizens and by the votes of hordes of new comers not lawful citizens."[78] In private, he said in April 1890 that the "Liberals stole the city and they intend to steal the County & Territory." Still, he wrote, "they are in the Hands of God as well as ourselves, and it seems as though the whole government were Determined to take away every right the Mormons possess but there they will ripen the Nation for the just judgments of God and if the wicked bring tribulation upon the Saints the wicked will not escape the just judgments of God in there turn."[79]

---

[75] John M. Whittaker Daily Journal, part 7, p. 24, Huntington Library, San Marino, California. In a meeting on February 10, the Twelve agreed that if the margin of victory turned out to be less than five hundred they could legitimately challenge the vote, since they had evidence to prove that "more than this number of People's Party voters were prevented from balloting through various tricks." If the number were over that, they agreed to leave the matter for later disposition. Cannon Journal, Feb. 10, 1890.

[76] Cannon Journal, Feb. 13, 1890.

[77] Cannon Journal, Feb. 18, 1890. In the Salt Lake County elections the following summer, the People's Party fused with a newly created Workingman's Party, made of gentiles and Mormons, successfully preventing a recurrence of the previous defeats. Cannon Journal, July 24, 29, Aug. 4, 1890.

[78] Journal History, Feb. 11, 1890, p. 2.

[79] Wilford Woodruff to William Atkin, Apr. 26, 1890, Woodruff-Atkin Letters, Utah SHS.

The fusion between gentile and Mormon political elements that took place in 1887 and 1890 also found its counterpart in the economic arena. In April 1887, leading Mormons such as Heber J. Grant, James Sharp, and Heber M. Wells joined together with gentiles like Governor Caleb West, William S. McCornick, James R. Walker, and Henry W. Lawrence to organize the Salt Lake Chamber of Commerce and Board of Trade. Agreeing to leave religion and politics outside the chamber's doors, the members promoted trade and home industries and worked to attract Mormon and gentile capitalists to the city.[80]

Nevertheless, Woodruff recognized the opposition to the Latter-day Saints on the part of the people of the United States. At the end of 1889, he wrote that "the word of the Prophet Joseph Smith is beginning to be fulfilled that the whole Nation would turn against Zion & make war upon the Saints." Eighteen ninety, he said, would be an important year both for the Mormons and for the gentiles.[81]

As the federal government continued its efforts to confiscate church property, Woodruff's prediction seemed fulfilled, though certainly not in the way he had previously thought. Throughout 1888, in proceedings before an examiner, the territorial supreme court attempted to define just what property the church would have to relinquish. Almost immediately, Attorney General Peters moved to confiscate the property transferred to local stake organizations, and the examiner included such property on the list.[82]

As Peters and Dyer worked to ferret out all the church's property, Woodruff staked the kingdom's survival on the hope that the government would stop at temporal property and leave its "sacred places of worship" alone. In mid-1888, it seemed as

[80] Thomas G. Alexander and James B. Allen, *Mormons and Gentiles: A History of Salt Lake City* (Boulder, Colo.: Pruett, 1984), 105.

[81] Woodruff, *Journal,* 9:74.

[82] Woodruff to F. S. Richards, Apr. 19, 1888, to Moses Thatcher, June 22, 1888, to John T. Caine, July 6, 1888, Woodruff Letterbooks, Church History Library.

though the church had won. The Utah Territorial Supreme Court's final decree, issued October 8, 1888, required Dyer to return the temple block to the church's Presiding Bishopric, providing the property was used exclusively for religious purposes as stipulated in the Edmunds-Tucker Act.[83]

The Supreme Court heard arguments in the suit early in 1889, but it did not render its decision until May 19, 1890. In that decision, written by Justice Joseph Bradley, the court by a five to

[83] Lewis Allen (Woodruff) to William Atkin, May 23, 1888, Woodruff-Atkin Letters, Utah SHS; Wilford Woodruff to George Teasdale, May 23, 1888, First Presidency Letters; First Presidency to John T. Caine, June 16, 1888, Woodruff Letterbooks, Church History Library; Wilford Woodruff to Daniel H. Wells, June 19, 1888, First Presidency Letters; Arrington, *Great Basin Kingdom,* 372; Grant Journal, July 23, 1888; Lewis Allen (Woodruff) to William Atkin, July 26, 1888, Woodruff-Atkin Letters, Utah SHS; Wilford Woodruff to John Henry Smith, Aug. 9, 1888, Woodruff Letterbooks, Church History Library; Wilford Woodruff to W. B. Dougall, Sep. 10, 1888, First Presidency Letters; Young Journal, Sep. 19, 1888. Despite the receiver's efforts, attorneys Richards and Broadhead worked out an agreement with Solicitor General Jenks to exempt temples, the tabernacle, and meetinghouses. The federal government would still confiscate temporal property but leave temples and meetinghouses in church hands. In view of the agreement exempting religious property from confiscation, Woodruff doubted that the church ought to take an appeal to the U.S. Supreme Court at all. With decisions in the Reynolds and Clawson cases behind them, in the opinion of many of its lawyers, the church stood no chance of winning. That being the case, without the appeal, while they would undoubtedly lose temporal property, they might lose less than if they fought through the Supreme Court, particularly if they succeeded in gaining the sympathy of the examiner appointed by the courts to assess the value of the church property. In addition, they could conceivably gain sympathy with other unpopular religious organizations, which might join in denouncing such legislation as subversive of the rights of the people under the Constitution.

By mid-summer 1888, however, they had decided against this course of action. After all, they did stand an outside chance of victory on an appeal on the constitutional question of free exercise of religion. Moreover, even if the church lost the case, the leadership calculated that they would still keep the temples and other places of worship. Wilford Woodruff to George L. Farrell, July 12, 1888, First Presidency Letters; Wilford Woodruff to Ammon M. Tenney, July 19, 1888, Typescript, A. M. Tenney Collection, folder 3, Church History Library. On this basis, the church completed the local negotiations and took the suit to the U.S. Supreme Court in October 1888. Richards Journal, Oct. 7, 1888; Woodruff, *Journal,* 8:520; First Presidency to George Teasdale, Oct. 11, 1888, First Presidency Letters; Lewis Allen (Wilford Woodruff) to William Atkin, Oct. 24, 1888, Woodruff-Atkin Letters, Utah SHS. On behalf of the schools, Charles S. Zane tried to break the settlement that Peters and Dyer had made with the church leadership, but he failed to do so. Lewis Allen (Woodruff) to William Atkin, Dec. 12, 1888, Woodruff-Atkin Letters, Utah SHS.

four margin sustained the government's allegation. Ruling that the church had engaged in illegal activities, it held the federal government completely justified in escheating the property.[84]

Significantly, however, and contrary to the expectations of church leaders, the Supreme Court ruling had left open the possibility of confiscating the religious property. In May 1890, however, confiscation seemed unlikely, since the church leadership had developed a good relationship with Frank Dyer and expected no problems on this score.

Then, in July 1890, Dyer resigned under fire, charged with malfeasance for the way in which he had managed the church's property, and the federal government began an investigation of his dealings. In his place on July 16, 1890, the federal courts appointed Henry W. Lawrence, "a bitter apostate."[85]

Throughout the negotiations between mid-1888 and July 1890, the church had come under increasing pressure to renounce the practice of polygamy publicly. On October 5, 1888, shortly before the church completed the settlement with Utah Territory and appealed the suit to the U.S. Supreme Court, Woodruff met with members of the church leadership and the attorneys. Dyer and Peters urged him to renounce polygamy as part of the settlement and save the church's property in the bargain. He told them he "would see the whole Nation *Dxxxd first*." Nevertheless, he worried about the situation of church members, particularly those in Idaho, where hundreds of Saints had taken the loyalty oath and registered to vote. Some had even withdrawn from the church to do so. All subjected themselves to prosecution for perjury, and although Idaho's governor had promised to pardon them, such actions added to the national uproar.[86]

---

[84] See *Late Corporation of the Church of Jesus Christ of Latter-day Saints v. U.S.* (136 U.S. 1, 1890). Woodruff heard the decision read on June 9, 1890. Woodruff, *Journal*, 9:97.

[85] Cannon Journal, July 16, 1890.

[86] Woodruff, *Journal*, 8:520; Lewis Allen (Woodruff) to William Atkin, Nov. 2, 1888, Woodruff-Atkin Letters, Utah SHS. See Young Journal, Oct. 5, 1888; Grant Journal, Oct. 5, 1888.

As events moved toward Dyer's removal, pressure continued to mount. On June 12, 1890, Secretary of State James G. Blaine gave a paper to George Q. Cannon, who was then visiting in Washington, for the "leading authorities of the Church to sign in which they make a virtual renunciation of plural marriage." Cannon's son Abraham said that his "feelings revolt[ed] at signing such a document."[87]

The Cannons immediately left Washington for Utah, but on June 30, instead of signing the paper, the First Presidency issued a significant change in policy, which they conveyed to church officials. Under the new policy, church leaders were told not to perform plural marriages in the United States and although they could still perform such sealings in Mexico, they might not do so "unless the contracting parties, or at least the female, has resolved to remain in that country."[88]

In August 1890, Woodruff and his counselors began a series of excursions on church business and on politics.[89] On August 11, the First Presidency left for consultation with church and political leaders in New Mexico, Arizona, and Colorado.[90] On August 25, they went on to the Hawaiian colony in Skull Valley. There, they dedicated the land as a gathering place for the Hawaiians who, unable to enjoy the privilege of temple attendance in the islands, had decided to emigrate to the mainland.[91]

---

[87] Cannon Journal, June 12, 1890.

[88] Cannon Journal, July 10, 1890. See also Shipps, "Principle Revoked," 71.

[89] On the political aspect of the journey, see Davis Bitton, *George Q. Cannon, A Biography* (Salt Lake City: Deseret Book, 1999), 308–11.

[90] Upon reaching Albuquerque by way of Denver, they stopped at the San Felipe Hotel, where they gathered in meetings with the Arizona stake presidents. After consulting with these officials, they traveled on to Santa Fe to meet with Governor Samuel B. Axtel, a friendly gentile, who had previously served as territorial secretary in Utah. From there, they journeyed north to visit the Saints in the San Luis Valley at Manassa, Colorado, then traveled on to Alamosa, where they boarded a train for Denver. On Sunday, August 24, they arrived in Salt Lake City. See Woodruff, *Journal*, 9:105–107.

[91] Woodruff, *Journal*, 9:108.

By the time the First Presidency reached Skull Valley, Henry Lawrence, with the apparent approval of the Republican administration in Washington, had begun to overturn the agreement on the temples between the church and the preceding Democratic administration. On August 30, 1890, John R. Winder of the Presiding Bishopric told Apostle Abraham H. Cannon that he had learned that Lawrence would soon attempt to confiscate the Logan, Manti, and St. George temples "on the ground that they were not used for public worship." Moreover, Harrison had reappointed U.S. Attorney Varian, who had opened the prosecutions under the Edmunds Act in 1884 and 1885 and supported Lawrence's contentions. On September 2, the court issued a subpoena for Wilford Woodruff to testify on the proposed temple confiscation, but he evaded service.[92]

On the night of September 2–3, 1890, Woodruff stayed at Emma's farm. The next day, he moved to the Gardo House, and at 2 A.M. on September 4, he and a "committee" left by Pullman car for Ogden, where they joined the Union Pacific train for San Francisco. Arriving in the middle of California's admission-day celebration, they had difficulty finding hotel accommodations. The ever-genial Trumbo found rooms for them at the Palace Hotel, and they proceeded to visit and negotiate with the California political leaders. After returning home, Woodruff issued the Manifesto.

Far from being a radical departure, the Manifesto conceded little more in public than the church leadership had already implemented in private. Statements by Richards, Penrose, and others (during the statehood constitutional hearings in 1888, prepared under the direction of Joseph F. Smith and other church leaders) had begun to move the church in the direction of accounting plural marriage a practice optional rather than

---

[92] Cannon Journal, Sep. 1, 1890; Woodruff, *Journal,* 9:109; Lyman, *Political Deliverance,* 135.

necessary for salvation. As the Manifesto indicated, the church leadership had already issued a directive prohibiting new plural marriages in the United States. If one interprets the Manifesto's statement about forbidding marriages prohibited by "the law of the land" in the light of the documentary context that "Congress" had enacted laws "forbidding plural marriages," which "the court of last resort" had declared constitutional, it seems clear that Woodruff meant the document at first to apply only to the United States. Moreover, as the Manifesto indicated, the church leadership reproved those who publicly encouraged plural marriages. Since 1882, the church had urged its members to order their lives so that they lived under the same roof with only one wife. Woodruff himself had become a temporal monogamist, living publicly only with Emma.

Subsequent events would cloud this understanding of the Manifesto. Particularly muddying the issue were the testimony of members of the First Presidency before a master in chancery hearing a case for return of the church's property and an interview in the *Salt Lake Times* in 1891 in which Woodruff said the Manifesto applied throughout the world.[93]

Had Henry Lawrence and Charles Varian not decided to proceed to confiscate the church's temples and other houses of worship, the clandestine pressure by the general authorities to stop open plural marriage in the United States might have sufficed for a time, particularly if the church began to share political power with non-Mormons. I emphasize *for a time,* however, since it seems probable that concerned gentiles—particularly Evangelical Protestants—would undoubtedly have ferreted out information on the new plural marriages.

In practice, however, the May 1890 decision of the Supreme Court, coupled with the Lawrence's and Varian's efforts, made

---

[93] Roberts, *Comprehensive History,* 6:223–26; Clark, *Messages of the First Presidency,* 6:211–17.

the proclamation necessary, as Woodruff indicated, for the temporal salvation of the church. On the day after the general membership approved the Manifesto in conference, Judge Zane essentially freed the church from any fear of further action aimed at confiscating the church's religious properties by accepting the declaration and announcing his belief in the honesty and sincerity of the church's "solemn declaration."[94]

Thus, the threat of religious sanctions, especially the loss of the temples, rather than pressure caused by the jailing of church leaders or loss of temporal property eventually forced the church into the public announcement of a condition that already existed. In the absence of such religious pressure, the church might well have continued to function even with the loss of temporal properties and with clandestine plural marriages performed in Mexico and elsewhere outside the jurisdiction of the United States. Adherence by church members to the rules allowing plural marriages only among parties who agreed to remain in Mexico might have stopped the parade of priesthood holders through the Utah and other territorial and state penitentiaries. Thus, Woodruff's statement in the Cache Stake Conference in 1891 was not an ex post facto rationalization for the act. Woodruff had every right to fear the potential loss of the church's temples and places of worship and with them the possibility of endowing members and performing the other living and vicarious ordinances necessary for salvation.[95]

What of the strident apocalyptic characteristic of Woodruff's 1880 revelation and of subsequent pronouncements? By late 1889, although Woodruff still anticipated the judgments of the Lord on the nation and upon those who warred against the Latter-

---

[94] Alexander, "Charles S. Zane," 312.

[95] Doctrine and Covenants (1981 ed.), Official Declaration—1, "Excerpts from Three Addresses by President Wilford Woodruff Regarding the Manifesto," 292–93. See also comment of Marriner W. Merrill quoted in Lyman, *Political Deliverance*, 136.

day Saints, he no longer expected the imminent fulfillment of these prophecies. No matter how fervently he continued to believe in God's eventual judgment upon the nation, he had also come to think that those events lay at some indefinite time in the future. By September 1890, it had become clear to him that God's wrath would certainly not fall on the United States soon enough to save the church from catastrophic losses. At that point, he faced the immediate problem of saving the structures that held the sacred space in which members could enjoy the blessings of the ordinances necessary for their salvation and the salvation of their dead ancestors. In a period of grace following the salvation of the temples, the church leadership could prepare for the future apocalypse by securing sovereign statehood for Utah.

In a more basic sense, however, Woodruff had begun to rethink and revise his conception of the apocalypse and second coming to see them as lying in the distant future. Certainly his understanding of these doctrines had undergone a considerable change between the wilderness revelation of 1880 and the Manifesto of 1890. No longer could the Saints expect God's judgments upon the nation and Christ's second coming to save them from unacceptable consequences.[96] Without this change in understanding, Woodruff would probably not have agreed to begin to cooperate with gentiles in politics or to confine new plural marriage to the Mexican colonies. Most important, without such a revised perception, he could never have understood a revelation such as the Manifesto, which essentially involved capitulation to national pressure for reform.

---

[96] For a somewhat similar situation, see Leon Festinger, Henry W. Riecken, and Stanley Schachter, *When Prophecy Fails: A Social and Psychological Study of a Modern Group that Predicted the Destruction of the World* (1956; reprint, New York: Harper Torchbooks, 1964). In both instances, there were increasingly intense proselyting efforts following the failure of the expectations of an apocalypse.

At base, then, the church leaders perceived not only the Manifesto but also the campaign for Utah statehood as religious. Both were tied to questions of ultimate concern—salvation for church members and their ancestors and preparation for the coming apocalypse, which they had by then come to expect at some indefinite time in the future.

In view of the events that had taken place before, the Manifesto became a way station rather than a beginning along the road to restricting new plural marriage and the sharing of political and economic power in Utah and the surrounding states. The oldest changes involved the sharing of economic power. After all, Brigham Young had cooperated in the construction of the Union Pacific; and the Bullion, Beck, and Champion Mining Company was a joint Mormon-gentile undertaking in which John Taylor and George Q. Cannon were heavily involved. Moreover, church leaders had developed close relationships with business leaders in enterprises as diverse as the Associated Press and the Southern Pacific and Denver and Rio Grande railroads.

Those among the church leadership such as Heber J. Grant, who believed in the basic justice of political and economic cooperation with non-Mormons would win the war and bring about fusion of the political cultures of both groups. That process of active political and economic collaboration had begun as early as 1887, and the leadership essentially codified the future direction of political activities in the 1889 Manifesto of the Apostles. The learning process continues today, because some church members still have not mastered the difference between giving advice on political matters and applying political pressure.

While inextricably tied to local political and economic life in the web of historical events, in the minds of church leaders, the decision to issue the 1890 Manifesto was at base religious rather than political or economic. The document announced to the world conditions that had already begun to exist within the Latter-day Saint community. In the most profound sense, the revelation was the religious side of a process of change that would continue down to the present time as the church abandoned attitudes that had served well while a persecuted sect but became irrelevant to a nationally and internationally prominent church.

The Manifesto of the Apostles constituted a way station along the road to religious respectability as well. In it, the church leadership repudiated the bizarre doctrine of blood atonement and proposed a new direction for church courts by denying their use in exacting civil damages.[97]

Thus, what began with the apocalyptic revelation of 1880 as Wilford Woodruff's religious odyssey became the church's journey as well. Woodruff and the church changed along parallel lines during the 1880s as both faced the same pressures and necessities. After 1887, as Woodruff became leader then president of the church, the lines increasingly converged. By late September 1890, Woodruff had reached the end of his odyssey, and he had prepared himself to receive the revelation that codified and publicly announced existing practice to the membership and the nation at large. In the process, he prepared the church membership for a new challenge in dealing with the pitfalls of increased public acceptance, which continues to the present time.

---

[97] On the degree to which this was implemented in practice, see Edwin Brown Firmage and Richard Collin Mangrum, *Zion in the Courts: A Legal History of the Church of Jesus Christ of Latter-day Saints, 1830–1900* (Urbana: University of Illinois Press, 1988), part 3; and Thomas G. Alexander, *Mormonism in Transition: A History of the Latter-day Saints, 1890–1930* (Urbana: University of Illinois Press, 1986), 102–104.

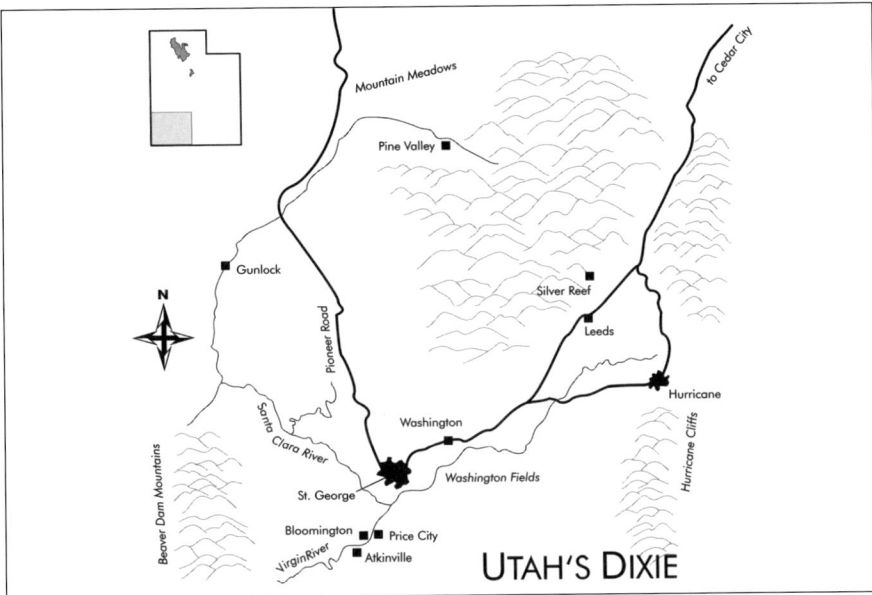

MAP OF SOUTHERN UTAH ("DIXIE")
During general conference in 1868, the William and Rachel Atkin family
received a call from LDS Church leaders to help settle St. George.

VIRGIN RIVER
The Virgin River was infamous for its terrible floods that destroyed
pioneer settlements and cultivated land in southern Utah.
Used by permission, Utah State Historical Society.

ATKIN HOME IN ATKINVILLE, UTAH
The William and Rachel Atkin family built a large limestone home
and cultivated the surrounding soil. Notice the American flag
in the background. *Courtesy Lynne Clark Collection.*

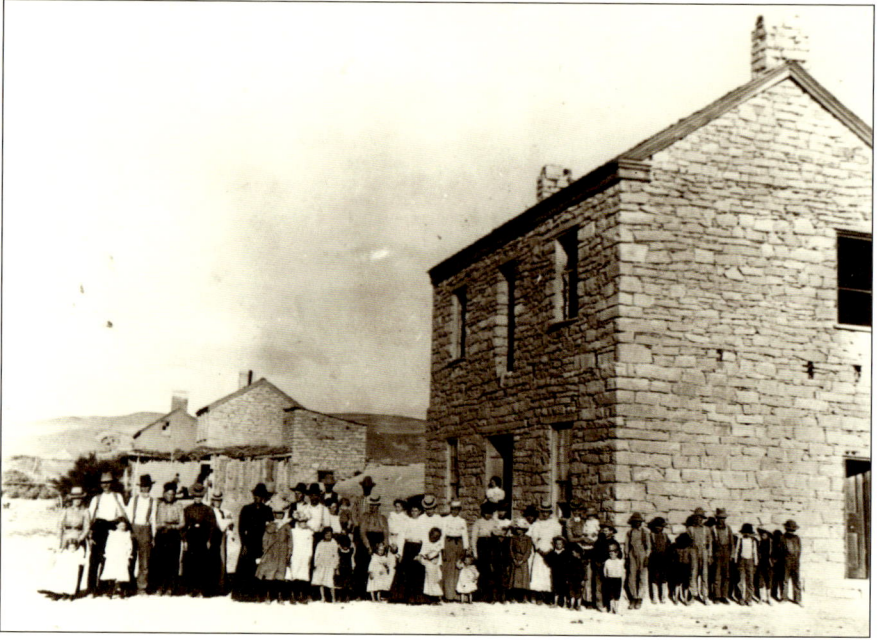

PRICE CITY, UTAH, RESIDENTS
Somewhat isolated from St. George, the Price Ward comprised
Latter-day Saint families living in Price City, Bloomington,
and Atkinville. *Courtesy Lynne Clark Collection.*

SONS OF WILLIAM AND RACHEL ATKIN
(*front row, left to right*) William Jr. (Bill), Joseph Thompson,
Henry Thomas (Ten). (*back row, left to right*) John Peter (Dack),
George Alma (Al), Heber Charles, Hyrum. *Courtesy Lynne Clark Collection.*

ATKINVILLE PICNIC
On weekends and holidays, crowds converged on Atkinville,
where they relaxed under shade trees, fished and boated on the pond,
and had picnic lunches. Visitors also enjoyed the Atkins'
ice-cold lemonade. *Courtesy Lynne Clark Collection.*

ATKINVILLE POND
This manmade pond in
Atkinville contained fish
and attracted a variety of
waterfowl. The Atkins and
their guests, notably Wilford
Woodruff, enjoyed fishing
and hunting here. *Courtesy
Lynne Clark Collection.*

JOHN TAYLOR
British-born Taylor was
president of the LDS Church
from 1880 to 1887. Because of
his practice of plural marriage,
he was forced into hiding
while sought by federal
marshals for the final years
of his life. *Courtesy LDS
Church History Library.*

Thomas Cottam home
Wilford Woodruff occasionally sought refuge at the
Thomas Cottam home in St. George. *Courtesy Lynne Clark Collection.*

PHOEBE WOODRUFF
Phoebe was married to Wilford for
forty-eight years. Federal marshals prevented Wilford
from attending her funeral. *Used by permission,
Utah State Historical Society.*

WILFORD AND EMMA WOODRUFF
In 1885, Wilford's wife Emma left Salt Lake City with
her daughter Mary Alice and joined her husband, who was hiding in
southern Utah. Emma and Rachel Atkin became good friends.
Courtesy LDS Church History Library.

ATKINVILLE PLAQUE
In 2000, members of the Atkin Family Historical Association dedicated
a bronze plaque mounted on a sandstone monument in honor of
Atkinville in front of the SunRiver Community Center,
St. George. *Courtesy J. Ralph Atkin.*

POLYGAMISTS IN PRISON
In January 1887, the Edmunds-Tucker Act escalated the
federal persecution of members of the LDS Church,
and several prominent church leaders were
arrested for practicing plural marriage.
Courtesy LDS Church History Library.

SHEEP SHEARING
The William and Rachel Atkin family owned
a large sheep herd that produced hundreds of pounds of
wool each year. Wilford Woodruff assisted with shearing sheep
while hiding in Atkinville. Identities of individuals in the photograph
are unknown. *Used by permission, Utah State Historical Society.*

WILLIAM ATKIN
Atkin and Wilford Woodruff
forged a deep friendship and
regularly corresponded for many
years. *Courtesy Lynne Clark
Collection.*

RACHEL THOMPSON ATKIN
Rachel helped care for many
prominent LDS Church
officials who sought refuge
from federal marshals in
Atkinville. *Courtesy
Lynne Clark Collection.*

MAY AND NELLIE ATKIN
May and Nellie, daughters of William and Rachel,
became favorites of Wilford Woodruff, who came to love them
like his own granddaughters while hiding in Atkinville.
Courtesy Lynne Clark Collection.

TABERNACLE STREET, ST. GEORGE
After William and Rachel Atkin left Atkinville,
they returned to St. George and enjoyed the conveniences
of city life and proximity to the St. George Temple.
Courtesy Lynne Clark Collection.

The Principle Revoked

Mormon Reactions to Wilford Woodruff's 1890 Manifesto

Jan Shipps

Although Latter-day Saint Eugenia Washburn later remembered, "[W]e were greatly astonished" when the Manifesto was issued, and although similar expressions of surprise can be found in the writings of others, it is still a mistake to conclude that the Mormons capitulated on the issue of plural marriage either suddenly or unexpectedly.[1] Woodruff's public announcement was issued on September 24, 1890, but quiet restrictions had been placed on the practice of plural marriage in the early part of that year. These restrictions possibly came even before the Liberals (the "gentile" party) won the 1890 Salt Lake City elections that were held in February and surely before the U.S. Supreme Court handed down its decisions in cases involving the confiscation of LDS Church property and the Idaho Test Oath; and also before the Cullom-Struble bill was introduced into Congress.[2]

This essay is an excerpted version of Jan Shipps, "The Principle Revoked: A Closer Look at the Demise of Plural Marriage," *Journal of Mormon History* 11 (1984): 65–77.

[1] Lorena Eugenia Washburn Larson, Autobiography, typescript, Genealogical Society of Utah, Salt Lake City.

[2] Edward Leo Lyman, "The Woodruff Manifesto in the Context of Its Times," paper presented at the annual meeting of the Mormon History Association, Dec. 1978, San Francisco, California.

Circumstantial and direct evidence indicates that these restrictions were not kept secret, at least from the Saints who might be described as part of the LDS "inner circle." In fact, enough was known about the church's policy of no longer officially solemnizing plural marriages or openly encouraging them to make the Manifesto such old news that the editors of the *Woman's Exponent,* who presumably ought to have been vitally interested (as they were all polygamous wives), ignored the story until it was published as a part of a report of the October 1890 General Conference activities.[3] More directly, Sarah Smith, a plural wife of Woodruff's counselor Joseph F. Smith, received a letter from her husband that he had written on the day the "pronuncimento" was announced, reminding her that while the Manifesto would "no doubt startle some folks," it would not startle her, as she would understand what was going on. An additional example is that of Martha Cragun Cox, who lived far away from the center of Mormon culture in southern Utah but had been warned by her bishop "months before" President Woodruff spoke officially to the press "that plural marriage was to be discontinued."[4]

In the great majority of the many survey treatments of Mormon and Utah history, the Manifesto is invested with so much importance that it is pictured as the agent of the demise of polygamy. Aside from the fact that the discontinuation of the practice had started before the Manifesto was formulated, there is ample evidence to indicate that the reality of bringing plural marriage to an end was much more complicated and that it took such a long time that the Manifesto of 1890 was superseded by other

[3] The first announcement was carried in the *Woman's Exponent,* Oct. 15, 1890. It was little more than a matter-of-fact account of what went on during the October 6, 1890, conference session when the Saints were asked to sustain the Manifesto.

[4] Joseph F. Smith to Sarah Smith, Letter, Special Collections, J. Willard Marriott Library, University of Utah, Salt Lake City. For the warning to Martha Cragun Cox, see "Biographical Sketch of Martha Cragun Cox, 1852–1932," typescript, 201, Church History Library, Church of Jesus Christ of Latter-day Saints, Salt Lake City, Utah.

manifestos before the process reached the stage in which the LDS Church can be said to have truly abandoned plural marriage.

First, assuming a cause-and-effect connection between the issuing of the Manifesto and the actual cessation of plural marriage requires an interpretation that pictures Woodruff's statement as a statement of policy. As its content shows, it was not that. The declaration started with a description of marital affairs in Zion in September 1890, which said that official sanction for plural marriages had already been suspended. It continued with a statement of the church president's own intention to submit to the laws of the land that forbade Saints to live "the Principle," plus his prescriptive advice to the Saints to do likewise. But it did not include two items that could have turned the Manifesto into a policy statement that would have been recognized as such by the Saints: there was no "thou shalt not, thus saith the Lord" at the beginning or the end, and the statement did not clarify the status of existing plural marriages. Consequently, the precise meaning of the Manifesto was ambiguous in the extreme, creating a situation marked by confusion and uncertainty.

In ordinary circumstances, such confusion would have been cleared away through time-worn LDS counseling procedures that make directions and information available to the Saints from the top of the hierarchical structure down through the ranks. In this instance, however, the normal administrative process that is designed to see that Saints "follow their file leaders" floundered on deep divisions over the issue of whether the practice of plural marriage should be given up, a division that fragmented the LDS hierarchy from the lowest to the very highest levels.[5] As a result, instead of clarification, the Saints received mixed messages from their leaders. This was such a difficult problem

---

[5] Kenneth L. Cannon II, "After the Manifesto: Mormon Polygamy, 1890–1906," *Sunstone* 8 (Jan.–Apr. 1983): 27–35.

that, in 1904, President Joseph F. Smith (who had succeeded to the position of president of the church in 1902) issued a "second manifesto," which had unmistakable "thus saith the Lord" overtones. Yet even that was not enough, and the ambiguity remained until 1905, when the church established its position with enough firmness to make it stick by dismissing two apostles from the Council of the Twelve and disciplining them for continuing to marry into plurality themselves and for encouraging others to do so.

Even in situations in which apostles, stake presidents, and bishops supported the discontinuation of the practice of plural marriage and made strenuous efforts to see that President Woodruff's advice was strictly followed, the matter was not as clear-cut as outsiders appear to have thought. The hierarchical and authoritarian character of institutionalized Mormonism, which led many observers to believe that the leaders of the church could compel the Saints to do their bidding, was then (and is now) balanced by the LDS doctrine of "free agency." Because this doctrine holds that when "the Messiah" came to redeem humanity from the fall of Adam, individuals became "free forever," knowing good from evil and being thenceforth able "to act for themselves and not be acted upon," the Latter-day Saints occupied positions of quasi-independence, poised between the necessity for obeying counsel and following their own consciences, which, in the 1890s, were consciences that had been formed in a world wherein plurality had been celebrated as a sine qua non. Without this notion of agency, Mormonism could not merit its privileged place in the divine scheme of things.[6] No wonder the Saints' response to the Manifesto and to directions to give up plural marriage was not as unanimous as their vote in conference might suggest.

---

[6] "Agency" entry in Bruce R. McConkie, *Mormon Doctrine* (Salt Lake City: Bookcraft, 1958), 25–27.

Not surprisingly, relief was probably the most common initial reaction to Woodruff's statement, even among wives fully committed to "the Principle." In her autobiographical sketch, the same Sister Cox who was warned about the impending abandonment of plurality noted, for instance, that "the issuing of the Manifesto had caused a cessation of strife."[7] During an oral history interview, Edith Smith Patrick remembered that it had relieved her parents of "all this persecution—or most of it."[8] In her account of her life, the articulate Annie Clark Tanner, whose birthday fell on September 24, remarked the happy coincidence that the declaration came almost as a present: "I can remember so well the relief I felt when I first realized that the Church had decided to abandon its position. For all my earlier convictions, a great relief came over me. At that moment I compared my feelings of relief with the experience one has when first crack of dawn comes after a night of careful vigilance over a sick patient."[9] And, in *Little Gold Pieces*, Juliaetta Bateman Jensen's story of her mother's life, the daughter recalled that her mother "said nothing, as usual, but she looked her satisfaction. What a sense of relief," Jensen continued, "must have come over her when the Manifesto was passed. There would be no more exile and night raids with their attendant anxieties. The future surely would be brighter."[10]

Brighter? Perhaps so, but for most polygamous wives, this did not occur immediately. The Manifesto raised more questions than it answered. It had been presented to the Saints in general conference and there accepted as "authoritative and binding." What

---

[7] Cox, "Biographical Sketch," 201.

[8] Interview conducted by Leonard C. Grover, July 1980. Filed in the oral history collection in the Charles Redd Center for Western History, Brigham Young University, Provo, Utah.

[9] Annie Clark Tanner, *A Mormon Mother: An Autobiography by Annie Clark Tanner* (Salt Lake City: University of Utah Library, 1969), 130.

[10] Juliaetta Bateman Jensen, *Little Gold Pieces: The Story of My Mormon Mother's Life* (Salt Lake City: Stanway Printing, 1948), 130.

did that imply? President Woodruff spoke about obeying the laws of the land: did that mean that new polygamous marriages could be solemnized where the laws of the land did not run—in Canada, for example, or on the high seas? Of more significance to those who were already polygamous wives in 1890 was that Woodruff's emphasis on no new plural marriages left the status of existing ones in limbo: were the covenants that bound partners in existing plural marriage relationships still valid? If not, was the institutional church willing to stand on the Manifesto as inspired? What, then, would the theological implications be?

Answers to these questions and many others all had to be worked out in an extremely tense political climate. For that reason, the LDS ecclesiastical leadership temporized, drew fine semantic distinctions, and sent mixed messages by giving different answers to different people on the one hand and saying one thing and doing the opposite, on the other. Tacit approval was given to some persons to have plural marriages performed outside the United States; others were reminded that polygamous practice had been suspended. Some polygamists were maintained in positions of responsibility, while others were abruptly released. Clarifying the intent of the Manifesto in Chancery Court, President Woodruff had to say that the discontinuation of plural marriage meant exactly that, including no continued cohabitation between plural marriage partners.[11] But at the very same time and for a long time afterward, many members of the Quorum of the Twelve produced offspring by multiple wives.[12]

---

[11] Several fine accounts of the immediate aftermath of the Manifesto are in print. In addition to the article by Kenneth L. Cannon II cited above, see Edward Leo Lyman, "The Mormon Quest for Utah Statehood," Ph.D. diss., University of California, Riverside, 1981, chapter 5; and Gustive O. Larson, *The "Americanization" of Utah for Statehood* (San Marino, Calif.: Huntington Library, 1971), chapter 13. The account of Woodruff's statement in Chancery Court and his commentary on it are found in Abraham H. Cannon, Journal, Nov. 12, 1891, Church History Library.

[12] Kenneth L. Cannon II, "Beyond the Manifesto: Polygamous Cohabitation among LDS General Authorities after 1890," *Utah Historical Quarterly* 46 (Winter 1978): 24–37.

Confusion reigned supreme, and in its midst several response patterns developed, within which polygamists dealt with the Manifesto; each of these patterns had important consequences for polygamists.

One of these responses was welcoming the Manifesto's message and using it to effect a fundamental change in lifestyle. When this response was adopted by polygamous husbands, it had a direct impact on wives who were more or less left to their own devices, not by choice but by the circumstance that their husbands refused to support them any longer, either emotionally or financially. Essentially the same response also could be adopted by any polygamous wife, as *A Mormon Mother* documents. Tired of running, hiding, struggling to maintain herself and her children, and playing second fiddle to her husband's first wife, Annie Clark Tanner used the Manifesto's message and her husband's refusal to accept it as justification for ending the relationship and going on alone to build a life for herself and her children.[13]

A response at the other end of the spectrum was adopted by "that class of people," in the words of Emmeline B. Wells, "who failed to see the Lord's hand," either in the Manifesto or in its acceptance as authoritative and binding.[14] All their efforts were directed to maintaining the practice of plural marriage, going, if necessary, to live in Mexico or Canada and in effect continuing to give all for "the Principle" as they had done in the 1880s. Accounts of their efforts are heartrending revelations of the cost demanded from plural wives. For a flavor of this response, note the words of Nancy Clement Williams:

> If ever Gethsemane was lived it was lived thro in my almost 4 years [in the 1890s] on that Dublan flat—6 miles from town—not

---

[13] Tanner, *Mormon Mother*, 141–336.

[14] Emmeline B. Wells, Diaries, 1890 Book, Sep. 29, 1890, Church History Library (hereafter cited as Wells Diary).

a telephone ½ the time and no teams around. Drunken Mexi-
cans coming when I was alone with small children. One son
getting his arm broken in two places; one daughter born and
died. A beloved sister from Diaz dead. [Truly she lived] in a
strange land among strangers. Only 5 teams to the funeral; no
friends to mourn with us. No one to speak of her [sister's] good
qualities as they had known her in life.[15]

The story of Henry Eyring's plural families in Mexico that is
recounted by Jessie Embry indicates that things were not always
this bad.[16] New support systems for plurality sometimes developed outside the United States. But one needs only to read Sam
Taylor's *Family Kingdom* or *Rocky Mountain Empire* to grasp
how difficult life was for those who adopted the response pattern based on rejection of the Manifesto.[17] For the plural families of John W. Taylor, Matthias F. Cowley, and a host of others,
life was demanding and strange in the face of the dissolution of
the elaborate and intricate network of practical and emotional
maintenance that sustained plural marriage in nineteenth-century Utah.

These two responses represented radically opposite attitudes
to "the world": the one accepting the standards and values of the
larger culture and the other rejecting those standards and values
out of hand. Yet a third response pattern—one that might be
called acceptance—allowed Saints to move into the larger culture while maintaining their peculiarity by staying individually

[15] Nancy Clement Williams, reminiscence and journal, printed in Kenneth W. Godfrey,
Audrey M. Godfrey, and Jill Mulvay Derr, eds., *Women's Voices: An Untold History of the
Latter-day Saints, 1830–1900* (Salt Lake City: Deseret Book, 1982), 368–69.

[16] Jessie L. Embry, "'To Lie for the Lord': The Effects of the LDS Church's Policy on Polygamy after 1890 on the Edward Christian Eyring Family," paper presented at the annual
meeting of the Oral History Association, October 1980, Durango, Colorado.

[17] Samuel W. Taylor, *Family Kingdom* (New York: McGraw-Hill, 1951); idem, *Rocky Mountain Empire: The Latter-day Saints Today* (New York: Macmillan, 1978). These two books
are written by the son of John W. Taylor. Both contain poignant accounts of the life of
his mother, as well as the lives of her children.

unspotted from the world. As interesting as are the often-tragic stories of the Annie Clark Tanners who found in the Manifesto an excuse to move away from the patriarchal order of marriage and the equally tragic accounts of the Martha Cragun Coxes and the wives of John W. Taylor who used rejection of the Manifesto as a means to enter into it more fully, this acceptance of the Manifesto was far more popular, and understanding it is far more crucial if comprehension of modern Mormonism is the aim.

In the fourteen years between the publication of the 1890 Manifesto and the promulgation of the so-called Second Manifesto in 1904, the lack of precision as to meaning allowed the Saints to work through the cessation of the practice of plural marriage in a manner that added strength to the Mormon movement. Practically, compliance with the injunction against new polygamous marriages was required, but—although it seemed for a while that all existing relationships could be maintained in name only with the husband providing financial assistance without enjoying connubial rights—time, distance from the lime-light, and extreme discretion allowed those who had entered plurality before 1890 to live out their lives in it.

Though all of this may sound easy, it was not. Taking this course, adopting this response pattern, called for a delicate balance between accommodation to the world and rejection of it. Plural marriage—actual, literal, living plural marriage—had, as indicated earlier, been absolutely central to the Mormonism of nineteenth-century Utah. Now its centrality had to be relinquished without undoing the synthesis of scriptural story and modern experience that made Mormonism live and flourish— and that could only be done if the Saints could be convinced that doing so was necessary.

A good way to look at what happened is to start not with plurality's demise but with its introduction into the community during Joseph Smith's lifetime, for that was not easy either. Even the prophet Joseph Smith needed revelatory reassurance to convince him that he was not about to commit adultery. Brigham Young wanted, at first, to die rather than to give his assent to the correctness of the practice. Orson Pratt was distraught, sent almost to the point of madness. And so on. Obviously, the introduction of plural marriage was a trial, a testing, that called on the Saints to exchange the comfortableness of American culture for life "in the Kingdom." It was a trial and a testing surmounted by a process not unlike conversion, as one individual after another moved over into polygamous practices. This process of conversion did not end in Nauvoo, Illinois, but continued in the valleys of the mountains, as innumerable diaries and journals attest.[18]

Now the process had to be reversed and Saints had to be converted away from polygamy. It did not happen collectively, but the process of being converted away from the principle clearly figured as the means by which plurality was given up. Juliaetta Jensen "more than once" heard her father say that when he went to the general conference in October 1890, he went with "some of his friends who had suffered exile and imprisonment and had determined to vote against the Manifesto." "But," said Jensen's father, "some power not my own raised my arm, and I voted to sustain President Woodruff in this matter. As soon as I had done it a sense of peace and contentment came over me."[19] Helen Mar Whitney wrote in the *Woman's Exponent* of "the late Declaration of President Woodruff which was sustained by Conference without an opposing vote." "When I perused the minutes," she said, "I did so with a prayerful heart and desire of the right spirit . . . and the testimony and spirit that came to me was strong enough to convince me that this step was right."[20]

---

[18] Lawrence Foster, *Religion and Sexuality: Three American Communal Experiments of the Nineteenth Century* (New York: Oxford University Press, 1981), chapters 4 and 5.

[19] Jensen, *Little Gold Pieces*, 130.

[20] Helen Mar Whitney, "The Opinion of an American Woman Whose Forefathers Fought for the Liberty That We Are Denied Today," *Woman's Exponent*, Nov. 15, 1890.

Zina D. Huntington Young said, "Today the h[e]arts of all were tried, but [we] evoked to God and submitted."[21] For, as Emmeline B. Wells said, "we must wait and see what the Lord has in store for us—we do not always know what is for our best good here and hereafter."[22]

The effect of seeing the demise of plurality in this context does not call into question the idea that the Manifesto and the end of the practice represented surrender and accommodation in some ultimate practical sense. But it does call into question the notion that things changed overnight and that the community gave up the practice primarily because they were "acted upon" by the federal government and the pressures of the larger culture. The responses of the community suggest, rather, that the practice played a crucial role in the development of Mormonism and that outside pressure was merely the catalyst, not the primary cause of this important change that moved Mormonism out of the pioneer period into the modern age in a form that allowed it to grow and prosper.

Plural marriage was introduced to the Saints, who, ever so slowly, converted to it in the early years, and the Saints gave it up in a comparably slow process that often involved "conversion" away from the practice. With remarkable symmetry, life was given to the practice and taken away from it.[23] This suggests that

---

[21] Zina D. Huntington, Journal, Church History Library, Oct. 6, 1890.

[22] Wells Diary, Sep. 29, 1890.

[23] It is interesting to note that the Wells diary cited above reports the presence of speaking in tongues and interpretation thereof among polygamous wives at this time of great trial; see entries for Mar. 15, 1890, and Oct. 3, 1890. A similar manifestation of spiritual gifts is noted in a selection from the journal of Ruth May Fox reprinted in Godfrey, Godfrey, and Derr, *Women's Voices*, 377. Reports of such phenomena are likewise reported in the selection from the diary of Patty Bartlett Sessions, also reprinted in *Women's Voices*, pp. 186, 187, 190, 191, 192, 194. Spiritual gifts among Mormon women obviously accompanied the process of conversion to plural marriage and then conversion away from this distinctive LDS marital practice. While reports of such gifts of the spirit are not restricted to these confusing and troublesome times, the presence of speaking and interpretation of tongues during the introduction and demise of plural marriage strongly supports the argument that the practice was religious to the core.

the practice was not a failed experiment; neither was it a frustrated religious activity whose continuation would be required of those who would experience the fullness of the LDS gospel. When it had served its purpose, plural marriage was slowly but nevertheless firmly subtracted from the panoply of doctrines and practices that combined in the nineteenth century to turn ordinary people into Latter-day Saints.

Part Two

THE PRE-MANIFESTO
CORRESPONDENCE,
1885–1890

LETTERS OF 1885

Salt Lake City,[1] Utah
December 13, 1885

William Atkin[2]

Dear Brother

Your interesting letter of December 5th is received and I read it with much interest.[3] Brother Atkin I highly prize the kind feelings you and others manifest in my welfare and safety. I look upon it as very providential that I was suddenly called to Salt Lake [City] to attend to the business of my quorum.[4] It gave me

---

[1] Salt Lake City, the capital city of Utah, is in Salt Lake County. Mormon pioneers settled it on July 24, 1847. It was called the City of the Great Salt Lake until 1868, when "Great" was dropped from its name. Since its founding, it has been the headquarters of the Church of Jesus Christ of Latter-day Saints (the LDS Church). *Merriam-Webster's Geographical Dictionary*, 3rd ed. (Springfield, Mass.: Merriam-Webster, 1997), 1034; John W. Van Cott, *Utah Place Names: A Comprehensive Guide to the Origins of Geographic Names* (Salt Lake City: University of Utah Press, 1990), 327. Many of the place-names in the letters that follow can be found in *Merriam-Webster's Geographical Dictionary*, but to avoid repetition, that source is not cited hereafter.

[2] William Atkin (1835–1900), son of William Atkin, Sr., and Elizabeth Wann: b. Mar. 27, 1835, in Empingham, England; m. Rachel Thompson Dec. 18, 1854, in Empingham; d. May 22, 1900, in St. George, Utah. William and Rachel had twelve children: Ester Ann, William Jr., Rachel Violet, Joseph Thompson, Henry Thomas, John Peter, George Alma, Heber Charles, Enoch, May, Hyrum, and Nellie Martha (see appendix 2). Jacqueline Williams Awerkamp, *William Atkin and Rachel Thompson Journal and Genealogies* (n.p.: privately published, 1976) (hereafter cited as Awerkamp, *Journal and Genealogies*); LDS Family Search Ancestral File, database available at www.familysearch.org (hereafter cited as LDS Ancestral File). The standard genealogical abbreviations "b." (born), "m." (married), and "d." (died) are used throughout the notes in the initial brief biographical sketch of each individual.

[3] Although Atkin family members preserved fifty-nine letters from Wilford Woodruff to the William and Rachel Thompson Atkin family, neither Atkin nor Woodruff descendants have been able to locate the correspondence from the Atkins to Woodruff. The staff of the Church History Library of the Church of Jesus Christ of Latter-day Saints, Salt Lake City, have likewise searched in vain for the missing Atkin letters. Ronald G. Watt to Reid L. Neilson, Oct. 25, 2000, letter in editor's possession.

[4] The Quorum of the Twelve Apostles is a body of a dozen men ordained to the office of apostle. As a group they constitute the second-highest leading quorum in the LDS Church, the first being the presiding First Presidency. Arnold K. Garr, Donald Q. Cannon, and Richard O. Cowan, eds., *Encyclopedia of Latter-day Saint History* (Salt Lake City: Deseret Book, 2000), 36–37.

the privilege of spending the first night and day with my wife
Phoebe [Carter Woodruff][5] before her death. This was on the
6th and 7th November. And on the evening of the 9th I had
an engagement to ride several miles out of the city to have an
interview with Presidents [John] Taylor[6] and [George] Cannon[7]
but before I left I felt impressed to go and visit my wife. I did, so
at about 6 o'clock I saw she was fading. I laid my hands upon her
and blessed her and I anointed her for her burial, kissed her, bid
her good by and sent my love to my friends in the spirit world.[8]
In 2 hours afterward she was dead. I did not see her after. I
could not attend her funeral. At the close of this interview I
got into a carriage and rode several miles and had a meeting
with Presidents Taylor and Cannon. The only one I have had
with Brother Taylor. I had two with Brother Cannon. On the
evening of the 6 November I spent the whole night in company
with the Twelve Apostles being 11 of us and the whole night was
spent in the trial of one of our own number which ended in the

---

[5] Phoebe Whittemore Carter Woodruff (1807–85), first wife of Wilford Woodruff: b. Mar.
   8, 1807, in Scarboro, Maine, to Ezra Carter and Sarah Fabyan; m. Wilford Woodruff
   Apr. 13, 1837, in Scarboro; d. Nov. 10, 1885, in Salt Lake City. Phoebe and Woodruff
   had nine children: Sarah Emma, Wilford Jr., Phoebe Amelia, Susan Cornelia, Joseph,
   Ezra, Sarah Carter, Beulah Augusta, and Aphek (see appendix 2). Ronald Vern Jackson, *Wilford Woodruff Family* (Bountiful, Utah: Accelerated Indexing Systems, 1980); LDS
   Ancestral File.
[6] John Taylor (1808–87), third president of the LDS Church, 1880–87: b. Nov. 1, 1808, in
   Milnthorpe, England, to James Taylor and Agnes Taylor; m. Leonora Cannon Jan. 28,
   1833, in Toronto, Canada; d. July 25, 1887, in Kaysville, Utah. Andrew Jenson, *Latter-day
   Saint Biographical Encyclopedia: A Compilation of Biographical Sketches of Prominent Men
   and Women in the Church of Jesus Christ of Latter-day Saints,* 4 vols. (Salt Lake City: privately published, 1901–36), 1:14–19 (hereafter cited as Jenson, *Biographical Encyclopedia*);
   LDS Ancestral File.
[7] George Quayle Cannon (1827–1901), member of the LDS First Presidency, 1873–77, 1880–
   87, and 1889–1901: b. Jan. 11, 1827, in Liverpool, England, to George Cannon and Ann
   Quayle; m. Elizabeth Hoagland Dec. 11, 1854, in Salt Lake City; d. Apr. 12, 1901, in
   Monterey, Calif. Jenson, *Biographical Encyclopedia,* 1:42–51; LDS Ancestral File.
[8] The spirit world is where Latter-day Saints believe the spirits of all mankind will dwell
   between death and the resurrection.

morning of cutting off from the church Albert Carrington[9] for adultery as you will see from the papers.[10] Now Brother Atkin I am happy to be able to inform you that I have had a happy time with my wives and children with the exception of the death and burial of my first wife and I have felt resigned to that knowing that she is far better off to be at rest than to live any longer in the midst of living and afflictions and persecution. She has worried about me ever since I left home and I would rather pass through the remainder of all my afflictions alone than to have her share it any longer with me. I have spent a good deal of my time with my family and friends since my arrival. I am happy to say as a general thing my family are all well except colds. I do not know that I can say anything more that will be of interest to you. We are looking daily now for the decision of the Supreme Court in [the] Angus Cannon[11] case.[12] We are now having quite winter weather—a few inches of snow and freezing hard nights. I have not heard from E[rastus] Snow[13] and company since they left for

---

[9] Albert Carrington (1813–89), member of the LDS Quorum of the Twelve Apostles, 1870–85: b. Jan. 8, 1813, in Royalton, Vt., to Daniel Van Carrington and Isabella Bowman; m. Rhoda Maria Woods Dec. 6, 1838, in Springfield, Ill.; excommunicated Nov. 7, 1885; rebaptized Nov. 1, 1887; d. Sep. 19, 1889, in Salt Lake City. Jenson, *Biographical Encyclopedia*, 1:126–27; LDS Ancestral File; LDS Family Search Pedigree Research File, database available at www.familysearch.org.

[10] See "Excommunicated," *Deseret News* (Salt Lake City), Nov. 18, 1885, 696.

[11] Angus Munn Cannon (1834–1915), president of the LDS Salt Lake Stake, 1876–1904: b. May 17, 1834, in Liverpool, England, to George Cannon and Ann Quayle; m. Martha Maria Hughes Oct. 6, 1884, in Salt Lake City; d. June 7, 1915, in Salt Lake City. Jenson, *Biographical Encyclopedia*, 1:292–95; LDS Ancestral File.

[12] In *Cannon v. United States*, 116 U.S. 55 (1885), Angus M. Cannon challenged the 1882 Edmunds Act that declared polygamy a felony, by declaring that he was not "cohabitating," or having sexual intercourse, with his plural wives and therefore was not guilty of unlawful cohabitation. The Utah Territorial Supreme Court ruled against Cannon. Edwin Brown Firmage and Richard Collin Mangrum, *Zion in the Courts: A Legal History of the Church of Jesus Christ of Latter-day Saints, 1830–1900* (Urbana: University of Illinois Press, 1988), 169–72.

[13] Erastus Fairbanks Snow (1818–88), member of the LDS Quorum of the Twelve Apostles, 1849–88: b. Nov. 9, 1818, in St. Johnsbury, Vt., to Levi Snow and Lucina Streeter; m. Artemesia Beman Dec. 13, 1838, in Far West, Mo.; d. May 27, 1888, in Salt Lake City. Jenson, *Biographical Encyclopedia*, 1:103–15; LDS Ancestral File.

Mexico. I got a good letter from Brother [George] Teasdale.[14] They still have hopes of getting land to settle on.[15]

> I remain your brother in the gospel of Christ
> Lewis Allen[16] [Wilford Woodruff][17]

My address for the present is inside Lewis Allen. Outside John Jaques[18] Box 321 Salt Lake City, Utah.

⁓

> Salt Lake City, Utah
> December 28, 1885

William Atkin

Dear Brother

Your welcome letter of December 20th was received last night and I having moved to a new place and having my time to myself

---

[14] George Teasdale (1831–1907), member of the LDS Quorum of the Twelve Apostles, 1882–1907: b. Dec. 8, 1831, in London, to William Russell Teasdale and Harriett H. Tidey; m. Matilda Ellen Picton Jan. 2, 1878, in Salt Lake City; d. June 9, 1907, in Salt Lake City. Jenson, *Biographical Encyclopedia*, 1:144–47; LDS Ancestral File.

[15] Beginning in March 1885, many LDS leaders and laity fled the United States to Mexico, where they hoped to practice plural marriage in peace. Legally acquiring land in Mexico was difficult, but they eventually settled ten colonies in Chihuahua and Sonora. Garr et al., *Encyclopedia*, 739–40.

[16] Lewis Allen is a nickname Wilford Woodruff assumed for his protection while hiding from U.S. marshals for practicing plural marriage. It was the name of one of Woodruff's schoolmates and neighbors in Avon, Conn. Wilford Woodruff, *Wilford Woodruff's Journal, 1833–1898, Typescript*, ed. Scott C. Kenney, 9 vols. (Midvale, Utah: Signature Books, 1983–84), Apr. 10, 1842.

[17] Wilford Woodruff (1807–98), fourth president of the LDS Church, 1889–98: b. Mar. 1, 1807, in Farmington (Avon), Conn., to Aphek and Beulah Thompson Woodruff; m. Phoebe Whittemore Carter Apr. 13, 1837, in Scarboro, Maine; d. Sept. 2, 1898, in San Francisco, Calif. Woodruff also had several plural wives and families (see appendix 2). Jenson, *Biographical Encyclopedia*, 1:20–26; Garr et al., *Encyclopedia*, 1361–65.

[18] John Jaques (1827–1900), assistant LDS Church historian, 1889–1900, and secretary to the First Presidency: b. Jan. 7, 1827, in Market Bosworth, England, to Thomas Jaques and Mary Ann Heighington; m. Zilpah Loader Oct. 31, 1853, in Liverpool, England; d. June 1, 1900, in Salt Lake City. Jenson, *Biographical Encyclopedia*, 1:254–56, 4:682; LDS Ancestral File.

I feel like answering it today. I highly appreciate your kind feelings in my behalf and the kind feelings of all my friends upon this
subject. I am doing the best I know how and then have to trust
in God. I don't know that I would be any safer in St. George[19]
than I would be at present. If the Edmunds Bill[20] becomes a law
it looks as though they would search through temple district of
course. We have got [to] watch the signs of the times and also
as the spirit moves. If they get crowding me too hard perhaps it
might be better for me to leave the country than to go to prison or
hide with family. I have got much too old to go to prison or hide
in the mountains for in either case I could not benefit the people.
The nation seems determined to do all in their power to destroy
the church and kingdom of God from off the earth. They never
will have power to accomplish that but they may have power to
distress the Saints until Zion is cleansed and the nations ripe for
the sickle which is ripening very fast. I don't know that I have
any news to communicate, only what you can get through the
press. It was reported that Lorenzo Snow's[21] trial was to come on
today. But I do not know yet. Remember me kindly to all your
family and especially that little granddaughter.[22] All my family
are as well as usual. I see some of them occasionally—those in
the north country I do not of late. (The devil is not dead. The
wicked priests and other[s] have not stopped lying yet; they will

---

[19] St. George is a city in Washington County, in the southwestern corner of Utah. It was settled by Mormon pioneers in 1861 and apparently named in honor of LDS apostle George
Albert Smith, the "Father of the Southern Utah." Van Cott, *Utah Place Names*, 325.

[20] The Edmunds-Tucker Act, passed by Congress in 1887, disenfranchised Utah women,
allowed for the federal seizure of LDS Church holdings above $50,000, and deemed the
offspring of polygamous marital unions illegitimate. Garr et al., *Encyclopedia*, 35.

[21] Lorenzo Snow (1814–1901), fifth president of the LDS Church, 1898–1901: b. Apr. 3, 1814,
in Mantua, Ohio, to Oliver Snow and Rosetta Lenora Pettibone; m. Harriet Amelia
Prichard Squire Jan. 17, 1846, in Nauvoo, Ill.; d. Oct. 10, 1901, in Salt Lake City. Jenson,
Biographical Encyclopedia, 1:26–34; LDS Ancestral File.

[22] Nellie Martha Atkin (1882–1963), daughter of William Atkin and Rachel Thompson: b. Aug.
1, 1882, in Atkinville, Utah; m. Franklin Livingston Burgess Sep. 6, 1900, in St. George; d.
Dec. 24, 1963, in St. George. Awerkamp, *Journal and Genealogies;* LDS Ancestral File.

keep it up as long as they can find anybody to lie to or until the Lord stops them.) We are having very pleasant weather. Here some are ploughing yet I attend no parties or public gathering. Cannot [be] seen openly, go nowhere only in the night, but it is like a prisoner's life but better than to be in the pen for obeying the Lord for he is as unpopular today as he was in Jerusalem but he will not be so when he comes again.

I remain your brother in the gospel
Lewis Allen

LETTERS OF 1887

Salt Lake City, Utah
July 29, 1887

William Atkin

Dear Brother

I have only time to write a few lines. I am in the city. Yesterday morning at 10 o'clock spent the day in the office. The great funeral of President [John] Taylor is held today in the Tabernacle.[23] A vast congregation. The procession has just passed. 7 bands of music, 103 carriages and buggies. 4 of the Twelve [Apostles] attended. I have 6 of the Twelve together and G[eorge] Q Cannon and Joseph F Smith[24] and D[aniel] H

[23] The Salt Lake Tabernacle is a landmark building on Salt Lake City's Temple Square celebrated for its turtle shell–shaped roof and amazing acoustics. Constructed in 1857, the tabernacle has been used to host LDS general conferences and funerals of dignitaries. Garr et al., *Encyclopedia,* 1211–12.

[24] Joseph Fielding Smith (1838–1918), sixth president of the LDS Church, 1901–18: b. Nov. 13, 1838, in Far West, Mo., to Hyrum Smith and Mary Fielding; m. Levira Annette Clark Smith Apr. 4, 1859, in Salt Lake City; d. Nov. 19, 1918, in Salt Lake City. Jenson, *Biographical Encyclopedia,* 1:66–74; LDS Ancestral File.

Wells.[25] I have seen Emma [Smith Woodruff][26] and family all well, I am well as usual. We had to leave our 2 colts at Elsinore[27] with Bishop [Joshua] Sylvester.[28] Could not travel as fast as we did. He will take care of them. I have no special news only what you get by the press. Remember me kindly to Sister [Rachel Thompson] Atkin[29] and all the family.

Yours respectfully
Lewis Allen

My address is John Jaques (outside) inside L Allen Box 321 S[alt] L[ake] City Utah

Please keep the contents of this letter in your own family as I do not wish my doing made public.

---

[25] Daniel Hanmer Wells (1814–91), member of the LDS Quorum of the Twelve Apostles, 1857–91: b. Oct. 27, 1814, in Trenton, N.J., to Daniel Wells and Catherine Chapin; m. Eliza Rebecca Robison Mar. 12, 1837, in Commerce, Ill.; d. Mar. 24, 1891, in Salt Lake City. Jenson, *Biographical Encyclopedia*, 1:62–66; LDS Ancestral File.

[26] Emma Smoot Smith Woodruff (1838–1912), a plural wife of Wilford Woodruff: b. Mar. 1, 1838, in Adam-Ondi-Ahman, Mo., to Samuel Smith and Martisha Smoot; m. Wilford Woodruff Mar. 13, 1853, in Salt Lake City; d. Mar. 4, 1912, in Salt Lake City. Emma and Woodruff had eight children: Hyrum Smith, Emma Minilla, Asahel Hart, Ann Thompson, Clara Martina, Abraham Owen, Winnifred Blanch, and Mary Alice (see appendix 2). Jackson, *Wilford Woodruff Family;* LDS Ancestral File.

[27] Elsinore is a town in Sevier County, in central Utah. It was settled in 1874 by James C. Jensen and other Mormon pioneers and named by an LDS Church leader after Elsinore, Denmark. Van Cott, *Utah Place Names,* 127.

[28] Joshua William Sylvester (1843–1925), bishop of the LDS Elsinore Ward, South Sevier Stake, 1877–87: b. Feb. 5, 1843, in Sheffield, England, to James Sylvester and Rebecca Nicholson; m. Christine Jensen Jan. 1, 1862, in Gunnison, Utah; d. May 31, 1925, in Eureka, Utah. Jenson, *Biographical Encyclopedia*, 4:626–27; LDS Ancestral File.

[29] Rachel Thompson Atkin (1835–1903), wife of William Atkin: b. Mar. 31, 1835, in Barrowden, England, to Joseph Thompson and Bridget Ann Philips; m. William Atkin Dec. 18, 1854, in Empingham, England; d. June 8, 1903, in St. George. Awerkamp, *Journal and Genealogies;* LDS Ancestral File.

Salt Lake City, Utah,
Sunday, August 7, 1887

Dear Brother and Sister Atkin

I feel disposed to devote a few moments to write a few lines
to you for acquaintance sake if nothing more. Of course you got
the D[eseret] News which gives you an outline of what is going
on. I thought I had written to you since I left St. George but in
looking over my journal I don't see it. Well we left St. George
with the two baby colts. They began to get lame and sick. We
stopped 24 hours on Fish Creek[30] to let them rest and doctor
there which gave me time to catch 54 trout while there.[31] When
we got to Elsinore we left both colts with Bishop [Joshua] Sylvester who said he would take care of them there. We drove 40
miles to Warm Creek and at 10 o'clock as I was going to bed I
received a telegraphic dispatch saying President [John] Taylor
was dead. I did not sleep much that night. Next day we drove 50
miles to Nephi[32] and there met a messenger from S[alt] L[ake]
City who wished me to take [railroad] cars in the morning for
the city which I did do. At 4 o'clock arrived in S[alt] L[ake]
City at 10 o'clock. Spent the day in the president's office. Met
some apostles and others. This was on the 28. On the 29 July the
funeral was held at the Tabernacle at 12 o'clock but the night
before I went to the Gardo House[33] and viewed the body of

---

[30] Fish Creek is formed from the western runoff of Mount Belnap of the Tushar Mountains
and flows through Piute and Sevier counties until it drains into Clear Creek, Utah. Van
Cott, *Utah Place Names*, 138.

[31] Wilford Woodruff took the opportunity to fish and hunt whenever and wherever possible.
For an account of Woodruff's adventures as an outdoorsman, see Phil Murdock and Fred
E. Woods, "'I Dreamed of Ketching Fish': The Outdoor Life of Wilford Woodruff," *BYU
Studies* 37, no. 4 (1997–98): 6–47.

[32] Nephi is a city in Juab County, in western Utah. Mormon pioneers settled the area in 1851
and named it after the prophet Nephi in the Book of Mormon. Van Cott, *Utah Place
Names*, 272.

[33] The Gardo House was the official Salt Lake City home of LDS Church presidents John
Taylor and Wilford Woodruff; it was located on the south side of South Temple, about
where the Zion's Cooperative Mercantile Institution (ZCMI) center is now found.

President Taylor. His body was viewed by thousands in the big Tabernacle from 7 o'clock until 12. I was at my office when the procession passed. It consisted of 7 bands of music, 102 vehicles, and a vast congregation. I met next day with G[eorge] Q Cannon and Joseph F Smith and the apostles and President George Q Cannon surrender[ed] into the hands of the Quorum of the Twelve Apostles the power and authority of the business of the church.[34] We met two days and I find myself introduced into a good deal of business. I went the night of the 28 and 29 to the farm. Met with Emma [Smoot Smith Woodruff] and the children; it was a happy meeting. They all send love to you. I have not seen any of them since Emma and Clara [Woodruff Beebe] went to Logan[35] Monday August 1. Clara got married.[36] They went to Smithfield to see Sarah [Brown Woodruff][37] and Bell [Woodruff Moses][38] and the children who were sick. I have heard nothing from then since only they returned home Thursday. Went to Provo Friday. Emma [Smith Woodruff] came home Saturday, so I hear, but [I] have not seen any of the family. I left Brother [William] Thompson at Nephi but he took her

---

[34] When President John Taylor passed away in 1887, senior apostle Wilford Woodruff presided over the LDS Church as president of the Quorum of the Twelve Apostles. Woodruff was sustained as church president in 1889. Daniel H. Ludlow, ed., *Encyclopedia of Mormonism*, 4 vols. (New York: Macmillan, 1992), 3:1420–21.

[35] Logan is a city in Cache County, in northern Utah. Settled by Mormon pioneers in 1855, it was likely named after mountain man Ephraim Logan, who died in the area in the 1820s. Van Cott, *Utah Place Names*, 232.

[36] Clara Martina Woodruff Beebe (1869–1927): m. Ovando Collins Beebe Aug. 3, 1887. Jackson, *Wilford Woodruff Family;* LDS Ancestral File.

[37] Sarah Brown Woodruff (1834–1909), a plural wife of Wilford Woodruff: b. Jan. 1, 1834, in Henderson, N.Y., to Henry Brown and Rhoda North; m. Wilford Woodruff Mar. 13, 1853, in Salt Lake City; d. May 9, 1909, in Smithfield, Utah. Sarah and Woodruff had eight children: David Patten, Brigham Young, Phoebe Arabella, Sylvia Malvina, Newton, Mary, Charles Henry, and Edward Randolph (see appendix 2). Jackson, *Wilford Woodruff Family;* LDS Ancestral File.

[38] Phoebe Arabella Woodruff Moses (1859–1939), a daughter of Wilford Woodruff and Sarah Brown: b. May 30, 1859, in Salt Lake City; m. Jesse Tilton Moses June 14, 1875, in Salt Lake City; d. Sep. 7, 1939, in Clearfield, Utah. Jackson, *Wilford Woodruff Family;* LDS Ancestral File.

home to S[alt] L[ake] C[ity]. Attended the funeral. Went back for his team brought my things to Emma [Smith Woodruff]'s here. Left his team there. Gone to Ogden[39] to visit his relatives at Clarkston.[40] Will be gone a few days, then return to S[alt] L[ake] C[ity], take his team and go home. It will be rather hard for him and me to part. He has been true and faithful to me. He has painted the outside of Emma [Woodruff]'s kitchen while waiting on me. I raised him some means to help pay his traveling expenses. Business will require me to stay in the region of Salt Lake County. It has multiplied greatly and it is an every day work. 4 of the apostles attended the funeral also D[aniel] H Wells. Marshals looked very sharp at him. Brother M[oses] Thatcher proposed to go but I would not permit [this], for he would have stood a chance to have been arrested and that would have created trouble. I am still in the enjoyment of good health but got no exercise but constant at work writing on everything etc. I want you to give my love and blessing to all your sons and daughter. Alice [Woodruff][41] enquired particularly about May [Atkin][42] and Nellie [Atkin] and sent love to all. I expect the ducks on [their] part and the quails will be glad that I am shut up in Salt Lake County. Our enemies are now again on the alert finding that we [are] again organized. The world expects to see Mormonism fall when a president dies but they forget that

---

[39] Ogden is a city in Weber County, in northern Utah. Mountain man Miles Goodyear settled the community in 1844–45 as Fort Buenaventura, then sold the land to Mormon pioneers in 1847. The settlement was named Ogden in 1850 to honor Hudson's Bay Company leader Peter Skene Ogden. Van Cott, *Utah Place Names*, 279–80.

[40] Clarkston is a town in Cache County, in northern Utah. Settled by Israel Justus Clark and other Mormon pioneers in 1864–65, it was named after its founder. Van Cott, *Utah Place Names*, 81.

[41] Mary Alice Woodruff (1879–1916), a daughter of Wilford Woodruff and Emma Smoot Smith: b. June 1, 1879, in Salt Lake City; m. William McEwan Nov. 16, 1897; d. Jan. 16, 1916. Jackson, *Wilford Woodruff Family;* LDS Ancestral File.

[42] May Atkin (1877–1927), a daughter of William Atkin and Rachel Thompson: b. May 20, 1877, in St. George; m. Amos Lathem Posey Sep. 1, 1897, in St. George; d. Nov. 4, 1927, in Tucson, Ariz. Awerkamp, *Journal and Genealogies;* LDS Ancestral File.

God lives. I pray God to bless you and all appertaining to you. I remain your brother in the gospel.

Lewis Allen

Salt Lake City, Utah
August 12, 1887

Dear Brother Atkin

Your kind letter of August 3rd is before me and while waiting for our breakfast this morning I will write a few lines in answer. I find myself very busy these days as all the work that was upon President [John] Taylor and council is now upon me to debate and direct in connection with my quorum and council but the responsibility rests upon me. There is 11 of the apostles now together including D[aniel] H Wells. We held meetings yesterday and will today from 10 o'clock through the day. I do not pretend to go to any of my family. Asahel [Woodruff][43] and Emma [Smith (Woodruff)] visit me on business occasionally. Fred Hopt[44] is dead, shot through the heart yesterday with 4 balls. Died going, as it is called. Called for dinner just before he was shot. Fl[ung] cigar out of his mouth just before the balls hit him. The agony is over in this world. It is just beginning in the next. You will see it all in the D[eseret] News.[45] Brother Atkin, Asahel is about to build him a home to put a wife in, in the S. E. corner of Emma's

---

[43] Asahel Hart Woodruff (1863–1939), a son of Wilford Woodruff and Emma Smoot Smith: b. Feb. 3, 1863, in Salt Lake City; m. Naomi Abbott Butterworth Dec. 14, 1887; d. July 2, 1939, in Salt Lake City. Jackson, *Wilford Woodruff Family;* LDS Ancestral File.

[44] Fred Hopt was executed for the 1880 murder of John F. Turner on Aug. 11, 1887, in Salt Lake City. Stan Larson, ed., *Prisoner for Polygamy: The Memoirs and Letters of Rudger Clawson at the Utah Territorial Penitentiary, 1884–87* (Urbana: University of Illinois Press, 1993), 150–51.

[45] "Hopt Buried," *Deseret News,* Aug. 17, 1887, 4.

lot. He wants to put a concrete or granite foundation 2½ feet or so to the top of the ground. Will you please state to me in a letter how that should be made? He is thinking of drawing the blocks of granite from the temple block instead of [— —]. How would that do? What preparation of lime is necessary with the sand? I would like it if you was with us to build that home for him, but that is out of the question. He wants to build about 35 feet square and have a dining room, parlor, bedroom, pantry, or butlery and bathroom and I thought if we can't work in 2 bedroom it would be a good thing. I wish you [to draw] on a small piece of paper you[r] views of such a building. He talk[s] of brick outside and adobes inside. Will it [be] necessary to line adobe partition walls or studding? Would it be necessary to line adobe walls to bind the building together? Give my love to Sister [Rachel Thompson] Atkin and all the family. Emma sends love to all.

> I remain your brother in the gospel
> W[ilford] W[oodruff] L[ewis] Allen

> Salt Lake City, Utah
> August 19, 1887

Brother and Sister Atkin

After a full day council on important business I seat myself at the table to answer your kind letter of August 14th. G[eorge] Q [Cannon] is reading on the floor. J[oseph] F S[mith] [is] reading the newspaper and resting. Has gone into the tithing office to see what two marshals are after there. So I have nothing to do for 5 minutes but write to you. Though I have no great news to give only we are busy framing a big Augean to make a state government and about a 1,000 other things. I get not much exercise only nights on which I call upon E[mma] [Woodruff].

Almost every evening but she is afraid to have me stop. Asahel [Woodruff] is making a calculation to build a home. He started yesterday to drive him a well. They drove down 106 feet yesterday [and] got a little water. 5 gallon a minute. I expect he has gone down 50 feet today, nearly 156 feet [total], and I shall look for a good stream of water tonight. I am going to see Brother [William] Thompson, [who] has been watching the whole operation yesterday and today. I learn that Marshal [Frank] Dyer[46] has gone to California; his deputies are doing some work in his absence but not as much as formerly. All our families are as well as usual. I got a letter today from Sarah [Brown Woodruff]. The children was getting better. All were improving but [she] was pretty well tired out watching with the sick. Work is increasing with me daily and I don't know as it will ever be any less. Give my love to all the family. Emma [Smoot Smith Woodruff] and all send love. I expect to take a ride with E[mma] soon 50 miles to Provo[47] to see Clara [Woodruff Beebe].[48] She has been quite sick but is better now. I don't think I shall ever be so busy but what I can answer your letters in several stops. Whether you can read them or not is another thing. I have clerks enough to write my letters and all my public letters but I scribble all my own private letters. I think I will have to change my present residence a while. God bless you all.

As ever yours
Lewis Allen

---

[46] Frank Hilliard Dyer (1854–92), U.S. marshal of Utah, 1886–89: b. Sep. 5, 1854, in Yazoo City, Miss., to Frank B. and Winifred S. Dyer; m. Ellen F. Tavey in July 1880; d. Mar. 25, 1892. Orson F. Whitney, *History of Utah*, 4 vols. (Salt Lake City: George Q. Cannon and Sons, 1892–1904), 4:281–82.

[47] Provo is a city in Utah County, in north-central Utah. Settled by Mormon pioneers in 1850, it was named after the renowned French Canadian trapper Etienne Proveau, who visited the area in 1825. Van Cott, *Utah Place Names*, 305.

[48] Clara Martina Woodruff Beebe (1869–1927), a daughter of Wilford Woodruff and Emma Smoot Smith: b. July 23, 1869, in Salt Lake City; m. Ovando Collins Beebe Aug. 3, 1881, in Logan, Utah; d. Dec. 29, 1927. Jackson, *Wilford Woodruff Family*, LDS Ancestral File.

~~

Salt Lake City, Utah
August 22, 1887

William Atkin

Dear Brother

Your very welcome letter come to hand with specifications of Asahel [Woodruff]'s home all right and [I] will say that the subject has been referred to Watson Brothers[49] builders. They are getting out a plan and I expect will build it. We have given up concrete and built the foundation of stone. Asahel wanted an artesian well to get water to make mortar so he got the well drivers. They work[ed] 2 days. The first got 106 feet [and] got small stream; next went down 35 feet further, 146 feet in all. Got sharp flow of water with 1¼ inch pipe stg with 30 feet in the air. Flows about 24 gallons a minute, good soft cold water. I thought Watson will build [— — — —]. I paid $70 for the well. I have moved my quarters from the office. Marshals a little too familiar. I am now as near the banks of [the] Jordan [River][50] as you are to the [Rio] Virgin[51] for a short time. I got a letter from Brother [Thomas] Cottam[52] [that] spoke of the sudden death of

---

[49] James and Joseph Watson, building contractors in Salt Lake City.

[50] The Jordan River flows north from the freshwater Utah Lake into the Great Salt Lake in northern Utah. Mormon pioneers named the sixty-mile-long river after the Holy Land's Jordan River, which flows south from the freshwater Sea of Galilee to the salty Dead Sea. Van Cott, *Utah Place Names*, 208.

[51] The Rio Virgin, or Virgin River, forms east of Rockville, in southwestern Utah, and flows two hundred miles to the southwest through the northwestern corner of Arizona and into Lake Mead, Nevada. Explorer Jedediah Smith is reported to have named the river after Thomas Virgin, who was mortally wounded by American Indians during his 1827 expedition. Van Cott, *Utah Place Names*, 385.

[52] Thomas Punter Cottam (1857–1926), bishop of the LDS St. George Fourth Ward, St. George Stake, 1887–96: b. Sep. 28, 1857, in Salt Lake City, to Thomas Cottam and Caroline Smith; m. Emmaline Jarvis Jan. 26, 1882, in St. George; d. Mar. 16, 1926, in St. George. Jenson, *Biographical Encyclopedia*, 3:353–54; LDS Ancestral File.

Brother W[illiam] Smith at the temple. I go to Provo tonight with E[mma] [Woodruff] and children to visit Clara [Beebe] for 2 days. I have been trouble[d] for a few days with diarrhea but keep to business. [Frank] Dyer got to California, I think he will feel better when he comes back. I look for removal of [Charles] Zane[53] soon. I think the signs are more favorable for state government and freedom than ever before, but all is in the hands of God. We trust in him. Give my love to Sister [Rachel] Atkin and all the family. Don't forget my Nellie [Atkin]. Alice [Woodruff] asks about her often. E[rastus] Snow I think is in S[alt] L[ake] County. We have lost [Brigham Young, Jr.?].[54] Can't find nor hear from him. All generally well. Owen [Woodruff][55] has a pony about the size of Hyrum [Atkin]'s.[56] He would like to run a race with him but I don't think they will this week. God bless you all.

As ever
Wilford Woodruff

---

[53] Charles Shuster Zane (1831–1915), chief justice of the Utah Territorial Supreme Court, 1884–88, 1889–94: b. Mar. 2, 1831, in Tackahoe, N.J.; d. in 1915. He was responsible for imprisoning hundreds of Latter-day Saints for their continued practice of polygamy in Utah Territory, so he was viewed as a hero by non-Mormons and a villain by the Mormons. Garr et al., *Encyclopedia*, 1394.

[54] Brigham Young, Jr. (1836–1903), member of the LDS Quorum of the Twelve Apostles, 1869–1903: b. Dec. 18, 1836, in Kirtland, Ohio, to Brigham Young and Mary Ann Angell; m. Catherine Curtis Spencer Nov. 15, 1855, in Salt Lake City; d. Apr. 11, 1903, in Salt Lake City. Jenson, *Biographical Encyclopedia*, 1:121–26; Garr et al., *Encyclopedia*, 1379–80; LDS Ancestral File.

[55] Abraham Owen Woodruff (1872–1904), a son of Wilford Woodruff and Emma Smoot Smith: b. Nov. 23, 1872, in Salt Lake City; m. Helen May Winters June 30, 1897, in Salt Lake City; d. June 21, 1904, in El Paso, Texas. Jackson, *Wilford Woodruff Family;* LDS Ancestral File.

[56] Hyrum Atkin (1879–1958), a son of William Atkin and Rachel Thompson: b. Feb. 10, 1879, in Atkinville, Utah; m. Elizabeth Eleanor McAllister Mar. 27, 1901, in St. George; d. Apr. 22, 1958, in St. George. Awerkamp, *Journal and Genealogies;* LDS Ancestral File.

Salt Lake City, Utah
September 3, 1887

Dear Brother Atkin

Last evening's mail brought me your kind letter of August 28th and also Lady Nellie [Atkin]'s which I read with much interest and which was quite amusing to my friends who heard it read. My health is good at present. I am where I can have exercise except while in council in the city but the fact is I do not have much time for hunting ducks or fishing there. We are in council for days at a time and a flood of business and have 10 to 40 letters in a day on private and public business and from 20 to 50 recommends[57] to sign daily so I have not much spare time. All the apostles are [at] council table except B[righam] Y[oung, Jr.,] and G[eorge] Teasdale. E[rastus] Snow's eyes are not as bad as represented. He can read his letters with glasses and he writes letters. I have L. John Nuttall[58] by my side as a clerk but he has from 10 to 30 public letters to write for me in a day so I still write my private letters to family and friends and leave them to translate my scribbling. Concerning Asahel [Woodruff] I will say he has got his trenches dug. Got a man hauling rock, sand and lime and will soon be laying up his foundation wall. Has finally consented to build with brick outside and adobe inside. After such a number of corner logs, a row of headers of brick which gives brick on to the adobe in a binder. As to his intended wife[59]

---

[57] Woodruff was likely signing LDS temple recommends—documents signed by priesthood leaders that attest to the personal worthiness of church members. Once LDS temples are dedicated, they are closed to the public; only members in good standing with endorsed recommends may enter. There are additional types of recommends for other church ordinances and priesthood callings such as missionary work. Garr et al., *Encyclopedia*, 1233–34.

[58] Leonard John Nuttall, private secretary to LDS Church presidents, 1879–92: b. July 6, 1834, in Liverpool, England, to William Nuttall and Mary Langhorn; m. Elizabeth Clarkson Dec. 25, 1856, in Provo, Utah; d. Feb. 23, 1905, in Salt Lake City. Jenson, *Biographical Encyclopedia*, 1:355–58; LDS Ancestral File.

[59] Naomi Abbott Butterworth (1864–1948), a daughter-in-law of Wilford Woodruff and Emma Smoot Smith: b. Mar. 1, 1864, in Braybrook, England; m. Asahel Hart Woodruff Dec. 14, 1887, in Logan, Utah; d. Nov. 16, 1948, in Salt Lake City. Jackson, *Wilford Woodruff Family;* LDS Ancestral File.

I am eating at the same table with her. She is 22 years of age, the best dress maker in the county and a noble woman. Well educated and refined, a splendid housekeeper. Can cook, make good bread, wash in black boots and will not marry any man who is opposed to polygamy for she believes in the principle. Give my love to Sister [Rachel Thompson] Atkin and all the family. I must write to Nellie [Atkin] so excuse my short letter. All goes smooth with me. No friction. God bless you all.

Your brother in the gospel
L[ewis] Allen

Salt Lake City, Utah
September 3, 1887

Miss Nellie Atkin, the Lady of the Lake

My Dear Love

I received your very interesting letter last night and I read it with much interest. I read it in the presence of apostles and a room full of people and that were much pleased that thought you was a brave young lady who was willing to do so much to defend the life and interest of the president of the church. But I don't wish to put my little Lady Nellie to so much trouble and danger. I have a large stout man[60] who goes with me everywhere night and day. Carries 2 pistols and a double barrel shotgun and says he will shoot the marshals if they come to take me. (Don't tell anybody of this.) So I am jolly well guarded. He drives a very fast team. He drove me to Provo with Emma

---

[60] The unnamed bodyguard was likely Charles Henry Wilcken (1830–1915), longtime bodyguard to members of the LDS First Presidency: b. Oct. 5, 1830, in Echorst, Germany, to Carl Heinrich Wilcken and Anna Margaretha Catherine Stoffer; m. Eliza Christina Carolina Reiche Aug. 10, 1853, in Neustadt, Germany; d. Apr. 9, 1915, in Salt Lake City. William C. Seifrit, "Charles Henry Wilcken, an Undervalued Saint," *Utah Historical Quarterly* 55 (Fall 1987): 308–21; LDS Ancestral File.

[Smith Woodruff] to see Clara [Woodruff Beebe] 50 miles in 5 hours and 30 minutes. The natural gait of the horses without any urging. Alice [Woodruff] enquires a great deal about you. She would be very glad to see you and so would I. If you should ever come into the north country with your father or mother you must go to Emma's and stop with them and with Alice and make them a long visit. I shall go and see you if you come in this county or if I go into the south I shall go and see you. You don't know how much I miss you buttoning up my shoes. I don't stop at home many nights so Alice can't button my shoes. And I have to ask some big man that will weigh about 200 lbs to button my shoes and he is so awkward about it I wish I had my Nellie with me. I would be glad to be with you and go to the garden and eat some of those good watermelons. Well I hope I shall see you some time if I should live long enough until you get to be a young woman and get married to a good Latter-day Saint.[61] I would like to come to St. George and marry you for I think a great deal of you. I don't know when I have ever seen as smart a girl and one that knows as much as you do in Utah. And I expect you will make a very smart woman. Give my love to your Ma and all the boys and May [Atkin]. You are blessed with a good father and mother. I pray God to bless you and make you an honorable mother in Israel.

Your Grandpa
Wilford Woodruff

---

[61] Nellie Atkin married Franklin Livingston Burgess on September 6, 1900, two years after Wilford Woodruff died (on September 2, 1898). Awerkamp, *Journal and Genealogies;* LDS Ancestral File.

Salt Lake City, Utah
October 8, 1887

William Atkin

Dear Brother

While our conference[62] is in full blast and Erastus Snow with others of the Twelve [Apostles] are at meeting and preaching and listening to my epistle[63] I sit down to write a few lines at my table to you. I have had one week [of] very hard sickness but am up again at work as hard as ever lately meeting until midnight. You say I ought to stop that. I would if I could but I don't know how. I expect you will think I am crazy or sun wild when you read in the [Deseret] News that W[ilford] W[oodruff], E[rastus] Snow, L[orenzo] Snow, F[ranklin] D Richards[64] etc . . . into the stand on Sunday and that W[ilford] W[oodruff] spoke to 10,000 people. But I expect you will read just such a thing. My epistle[65] is being read today. It will take 1½ hours and I cannot write much now. I have two letters of yours unanswered before me; the last was September 14. But I hardly have time these days to read a letter or answer it only as I find a few moments. Leisure as I have now to answer half a dozen letters in 30 minutes and leave my friends to read the best they can. Give my love to all the family and accept mine. The conference

---

[62] Latter-day Saints have held conferences, or churchwide meetings, generally in April and October, since the beginnings of Mormonism. The Fifty-eighth Semi-annual LDS Church Conference was held in Salt Lake City, Oct. 6–9, 1887.

[63] As a federal fugitive, Woodruff could not attend general conference, so he had his message read to the general assembly in his absence. See "General Conference," *Deseret News,* Oct. 12, 1887, 612–13, 620–21.

[64] Franklin Dewey Richards (1821–99), member of the LDS Quorum of the Twelve Apostles, 1849–99: b. Apr. 2, 1821, in Richmond, Mass., to Phineas Richards and Wealthy Dewey: m. Jane Synder Dec. 18, 1842, in Job Creek, Ill.; d. Dec. 9, 1899, in Ogden, Utah. Jenson, *Biographical Encyclopedia,* 1:115–21; Garr et al., *Encyclopedia,* 1020–21; LDS Ancestral File.

[65] For the text of his address, see Wilford Woodruff, "An Epistle to the Members of the Church of Jesus Christ of Latter-day Saints," *Deseret News,* Oct. 12, 1887, 616–17, 624.

is so full the Tabernacle will not hold them. A big meeting and big times, more than I can talk about today. I have my friends and many homes open to me. I don't know but I have forgotten how to talk to the people; I think by tomorrow 4 o'clock [I] shall find out. (When sharks are caught in a net can they hurt anybody until they are let out.) God bless you all and your family.

As ever yours
Lewis Allen

Salt Lake City, Utah
November 24, 1887

William Atkin

Dear Brother

Well Emma [Smith Woodruff] has gone up town to get Beulah [Woodruff Beatte][66] and some of the children and while the family is cooking I will spend a few moments to answer your letter of November 18th which has just been handed me. Well lightning has just struck. [Frank] Dyer the marshal came yesterday [and] took possession of all our office.[67] The president's office took up the desk [and] took the [keys] and turned us all out. We left just in time. I am happy keeping Thanksgiving. You will see by the [Deseret] News they took possession of the temple block, tithing office, Gardo [House], history office.[68] We

---

[66] Beulah Augusta Woodruff Beatte (1851–1905), a daughter of Wilford Woodruff and Phoebe Whittemore Carter: b. July 19, 1851, in Salt Lake City; m. Sidney Hampton Beatte June 30, 1868; d. Jan. 13, 1905, in Salt Lake City. Jackson, *Wilford Woodruff Family;* LDS Ancestral File.

[67] U.S. Marshal Frank Dyer seized the LDS First Presidency's Salt Lake City office, leaving two lawmen to prevent unauthorized entrance on November 23, 1887. Andrew Jenson, *Church Chronology* (Salt Lake City: Deseret News, 1899), 155.

[68] See "President's Office Seized," *Deseret News,* Nov. 30, 1887, 724.

give $1 a month for the temple block and $200 dollar a month for the tithing office and history office. They demand all our money, bank notes, but miss much as they are on the *warpath*. They must find those if they can. I don't know where the end is but it must come to an end some time; there is no road without a turn. My family are generally well. I have suffered the most of anyone for a month with a severe cold [in] my lung[s]. I have coughed some of the time every minute for 24 hours without any sleep but I am better now though still cough some but feel some better. Attend to business. Sat up some of the time until near midnight talking to the lawyers and I can hardly find two of them who agree upon our case. Well you get all the news in the paper upon our case so I need not say anything more upon the subject. Give my love to Sister [Rachel Thompson] Atkin and all the children not forgetting Nellie [Atkin]. I have just finished a carp pond on the northeast corner of our lot. 40 × 45 feet also 4 feet of water will hold 200 carp well.

As ever yours. Emma and all send love.
Lewis Allen

Salt Lake City, Utah
December 23, 1887

Dear Brother and Sister Atkin

I got Brother William [Atkin]'s letter of the 16th. I was glad to hear from you and that all was well with you. I am thankful to say that I have got over my cold and cough. It followed me very hard for one month but I enjoy very good health at present. My daughter Clara [Woodruff Beebe] came from Provo with her husband to attend Asahel [Woodruff]'s wedding party and

she was taken sick, and went down to death's door and it looked
as though we would lose [her] but by administration[69] and nurs-
ing she has got up again. Wilford [Woodruff]'s son Wilford
[Woodruff, Jr.,][70] broke his leg but it is doing well now but Julia
[Spencer Woodruff],[71] his wife, is very sick with milk sickness.[72]
Her left leg is swollen as full as skin can hold up to her hip. I have
administered to her, and a Dr. [Ellen] Ferguson,[73] a woman, has
attended on her but she is still very poorly [and has] not been
able to get up since her child was born. My daughter [Phoebe]
Arabella [Woodruff] Moses is still quite poorly but much better
than she was. We are getting along in our business as well as we
can except Marshal [Frank] Dyer has gone East and all is still
at present. Emma [Smith Woodruff] is well as usual and sends
love to all the family. Give my love to all the children and tell
Nellie [Atkin] I don't forget her. Alice [Woodruff] is with her
mother and keeping house for her. Asahel [Woodruff] has got
into his house with his wife and all cozy and happy. His house
cost some $1,800 and $500 to furnish it. It is a nice building and
well furnished. G[eorge] Q C[annon] and J[oseph] F S[mith]

---

[69] Administration refers to a healing blessing offered by worthy LDS men through the authority of the Melchizedek Priesthood and by the laying on of hands. Ludlow, *Encyclopedia
of Mormonism,* 3:1308–1309.

[70] Wilford Woodruff, Jr. (1840–1921), a son of Wilford Woodruff and Phoebe Whittemore
Carter: b. Mar. 22, 1840, in Montrose, Iowa; m. Emily Jane Smith Oct. 12, 1867, in Salt
Lake City; d. May 6, 1921, in Salt Lake City. Jenson, *Biographical Encyclopedia,* 1:616–17;
Jackson, *Wilford Woodruff Family;* LDS Ancestral File.

[71] Julia Spencer Woodruff (1856–95), a daughter-in-law of Wilford Woodruff and Phoebe
Whittemore Carter: b. May 6, 1856, in Nephi, Utah, to George Spencer and Emily
Brown Bush; m. Wilford Woodruff, Jr., May 25, 1879, in St. George; d. Feb. 1, 1895, in
Salt Lake City. Jackson, *Wilford Woodruff Family;* LDS Ancestral File.

[72] Milk sickness, or tremetol poisoning, is a disease contracted by eating meat or dairy prod-
ucts from plant-poisoned cattle.

[73] Ellen Brooke Ferguson (1844–1920), Utah pioneer physician: b. Apr. 10, 1844, in Cambridge, England, to William Lombe Brooke and his wife; m. William Ferguson in 1857
in England; d. Mar. 17, 1920, in New York. Whitney, *History of Utah,* 4:602–604; Vicky
Burgess-Olson, ed., *Sister Saints* (Provo, Utah: Brigham Young University Press, 1978),
327–37.

are with me and well and wish to be remembered. They are much help to me.

I remain as ever your brother
L[ewis] Allen

LETTERS OF 1888

Salt Lake City, Utah
January 20, 1888

William Atkin

Dear Brother

I have received your letter of the [January] 8th and read with interest as I do all your letters. I think it is quite an uncommon thing for you to have ice 10 inches thick or 6 inches.[74] The thought struck me about the health of ice for drinking taken from a pond that you would not consider the water suitable for drinking. The ice formed from that water would be of the same nature. Of course the ice would be suitable for any cooking purposes and it might not be injurious to drink. My health is very good at present as is the case with the brethren with me. I think business rather grows upon us with 20 or 40 letters daily. Our state government, our legislature, Congress, our lawsuit,[75] and all church affairs taken together keep me very busy. (Private[ly,] I was very sorry to learn of D[avid] H Cannon's[76] affairs. I was in hopes he had age and

---

[74] The Atkins lived in southwestern Utah and enjoyed mild winters and hot summers. Still, they were able to harvest ice blocks from frozen ponds during the coldest months of the year.

[75] *The Late Corporation of the Mormon Church v. United States*, a lawsuit filed against the federal seizure of LDS Church property per the Edmunds-Tucker Act of 1887.

[76] David Henry Cannon (1838–1924), president of the LDS St. George Temple, 1893–1924: b. Apr. 23, 1838, in Liverpool, England, to George Cannon and Ann Quayle; m. Wilhelmina L. Mousley Feb. 15, 1859, in Salt Lake City; d. Dec. 24, 1924, in St. George. LDS Ancestral File.

experience enough to keep out of such scrapes as that.) As to Sullivan I don't know much about his operation. Maybe in his line. I don't think he is much of a Saint. Our lawsuit has not done much of late and [I] expect something will soon be done in it. We are having very cold weather. Thermometer 16 degrees below zero in Salt Lake [City,] 24 in Ogden, 30 in Cache [Valley,][77] and 40 and 45 in Bear Lake.[78] There is hardly snow enough here for sleighing, still some sleighs run. My daughter Clara [Woodruff Beebe] is both better and worse—has very poor suffering spots then gets better. Julia [Spencer Woodruff] is getting up again slowly [and] is about the house. Wilford's oldest son Wilford [Woodruff, Jr.,] who broke his leg, is around again. Give my love to Sister [Rachel Thompson] Atkin, my Nellie [Atkin] and all the boys.

I remain as ever yours
L[ewis] Allen

Salt Lake City, Utah
February 13, 1888

William Atkin

Dear Brother
Your letter of the 6[th of February] is just received which I read with interest. I was very sorry to hear of William [Atkin, Jr.]'s[79]

[77] Cache Valley is a region in north-central Utah. Before Mormon settlers colonized the region, mountain men and American Indians met there to exchange furs and goods. Logan, Hyrum, Wellsville, and Smithfield are all established communities in the valley. Van Cott, *Utah Place Names*, 61.

[78] Bear Lake is a freshwater lake about twenty-two miles long and between two to six miles wide on the Utah and Idaho border. The Hudson's Bay Company's Donald McKenzie had named the lake by 1819 because of the many bears in the area. Van Cott, *Utah Place Names*, 23–24.

[79] William Atkin, Jr. (1859–1941), a son of William Atkin and Rachel Thompson: b. Mar. 23, 1859, in Ashland, Penn.; m. Rossetta Stucki (1856–1920) Oct. 2, 1879, in St. George; d. Jan. 8, 1941, in St. George. Awerkamp, *Journal and Genealogies;* LDS Ancestral File.

accident. I hope it will not end in any lasting injury to him but it is a serious thing. Give him my love and tell him I hope he will soon get well and that he will not follow my example any further as far as broken bones are concerned.[80] My health is good at present as is most of my family. Clara [Woodruff Beebe] has got better able to be about the house. Julia [Spencer Woodruff] is around again about as usual. [Phoebe] Bell [Woodruff] Moses has got better so all my sick are better. The election is going on today. Some scratching I expect when you read the governor's[81] speech before the liberals; you will think he is about to join the church but he has not been baptized yet.[82] No man a month ago could have dreamed there would ever have been such a split in [the] ring as now but [you] will read all the music in the [Deseret] News. Our lawsuit is becoming quite salty. They seem determined to get all the church property they can. Emma [Smith Woodruff], Alice [Woodruff], and all join me in love to you, Sister [Rachel Thompson] Atkin, and all the family. Nellie [Woodruff],[83] Emma's oldest, has a daughter,[84] which makes

---

[80] Wilford Woodruff was "beset with an unusual number of accidents during his life. He suffered broken bones in his arms and legs, split his foot with an ax, was bitten by a rabid dog, and was crushed and pinned by falling trees. He nearly lost his life from blood poisoning when he accidentally cut his arm while skinning an ox that had died of poison. He survived the wreck of a speeding train, nearly drowned, was frozen and scalded, and suffered several severe illnesses." Ludlow, *Encyclopedia of Mormonism*, 4:1581.

[81] Caleb Walton West (1844–1909), governor of Utah Territory, 1886–88, 1893–96: b. May 25, 1844, in Cynthiana, Ky.; m. Nancy Frazer; d. Jan. 25, 1909. Allan Kent Powell, ed., *Utah History Encyclopedia* (Salt Lake City: University of Utah Press, 1994), 549–50.

[82] During the 1888 Salt Lake City election, the LDS-backed People's Party sought to include the Liberal Party on their ticket to better represent the electorate of Utah. This "fusion movement," backed by Governor Caleb West, ultimately won the February election, but not before coming under fire by some in the community. Orson F. Whitney, *Popular History of Utah* (Salt Lake City: Deseret News, 1916), 458–59.

[83] Emma Minilla Woodruff (1860–1905), a daughter of Wilford Woodruff and Emma Smoot Smith: b. July 4, 1860, in Salt Lake City; m. Henry Azmon Woodruff (1855–1939) Jan. 15, 1880, in Salt Lake City; d. Nov. 30, 1905, in Vernal. Jackson, *Wilford Woodruff Family*; LDS Ancestral File.

[84] Emma Estella Woodruff (1888–1913), a granddaughter of Wilford Woodruff and Emma Smoot Smith: b. Jan. 31, 1888, in Vernal to Henry Azmon Woodruff and Emma Minilla Woodruff; d. Mar. 5, 1913, in Vernal. Jackson, *Wilford Woodruff Family;* LDS Ancestral File.

the first grand daughter to her. Susan [Woodruff Scholes]'s[85] oldest daughter, Eugenia [Scholes,][86] has a son, which makes me a great great grandfather. I pray God to bless you all and heal up William.

As ever your
L[ewis] Allen

Salt Lake City, Utah
March 7, 1888

William Atkin

Dear Brother

Your letter of February 26th is before me. I have read it with much interest. Yes I have [passed] my birth.[87] I don't feel much older for it. I am glad you are all as well as you are. I hope William [Atkin, Jr.,] will get over a serious accident. A Brother Robert [Stewart][88] was mashed up at the depot while coupling cars 2 days ago. My family are well as usual. Clara [Woodruff Beebe] is about [the] house again. Julia [Spencer Woodruff] is at work and [Phoebe] Bell [Woodruff] Moses is much better. I am pretty well for a man of my age and such exercise taken as I have had of late. I was in council Tuesday night till 12 o'clock with the 12 [Apostles] and legislature and last night the meeting

---

[85] Susan Cornelia Woodruff (1843–97), a daughter of Wilford Woodruff and Phoebe Whittemore Carter: b. July 25, 1843, in Nauvoo, Ill.; m. Robert Scholes Jan. 30, 1859; d. Oct. 6, 1897, in Sioux City, Iowa. Jackson, *Wilford Woodruff Family;* LDS Ancestral File.

[86] Eugenia Amelia Scholes (1860–99), a granddaughter of Wilford Woodruff and Emma Smoot Smith: b. May 21, 1860, in Salt Lake City to Robert Scholes and Susan Cornelia Woodruff; d. July 21, 1899. Jackson, *Wilford Woodruff Family;* LDS Ancestral File.

[87] Wilford Woodruff, born on March 1, 1807, had just celebrated his eighty-third birthday.

[88] For an account of this tragedy, see "Robert Stewart Killed," *Salt Lake Tribune,* Jan. 7, 1888.

held till one o'clock but I stayed in my room to rest. I shall have some relief when the legislature closes but our Washington affairs, state government, with church business and our lawsuit gives me all the labor and care I can attend to. In fact I marvel that I can keep around but I do. I made a mistake in directing one of your letters to Unionville instead of Bloomington as I was writing to that place when your letter was dated. Most all my letters are copied by clerks except some few I write to special friends and I don't have time to get them copied. Excuse the short letter. Give my love to Sister [Rachel Thompson] Atkin and all the sons and daughters. And I thank you all for all your kind wishes and good deeds.

Still your brother
Lewis Allen

[Upside down] I have no trouble with my tumor [though] it still grows. I still suffer with colds and cough most of the time.

Salt Lake City, Utah
April 4, 1888

William Atkin

Dear Brother

I received a letter from Brother [John] McAllister[89] and I judged he was at your home, and perhaps several other brethren, and so I have written several letters and enclosed [them] direct to you, which I wish you to distribute when you have a chance

89 John Daniel Thompson McAllister (1827–1910), president of the LDS St. George Stake, 1877–88: b. Feb. 19, 1827, to William J. F. McAllister and Eliza Thompson in Lewis, Del.; m. Ellen Handley July 5, 1847, in Philadelphia; d. Jan. 18, 1910, in St. George. Jenson, *Biographical Encyclopedia*, 1:334; LDS Ancestral File.

as they may be with you—and if they are not, send [the letters] to them when you have a chance. It seems that you was not inspired any too soon to build that stone room[90] that I occupied as it may accommodate a number of men. I am still busy and crowded with work. My health is pretty good at present. I was glad to hear that William [Atkin, Jr.,] was recovering from his hurt. I hope he will get well again. I want you to give my love to Sister [Rachel Thompson] Atkin and all the boys and girls. Sister Atkin has waited upon me like a mother and I cannot forget it. I would like to see you all again. Our state suit is still going on. I don't know what the end would be. If you ever come to the county come and see me and I will do the same by you. I would like to go over your place once more and see how things look over the farm and pond etc. I hope you may prosper in all you do. Conference is upon us.[91] I shall not attend this year. I shall write but a short epistle this conference.[92] You will now have to watch for a new kind of black duck. I pray God to bless you for all your kindness to all men under ground[93] and above ground.

Your brother
L[ewis] Allen

---

[90] The Atkin family added on a limestone room to their house that they named the "Wilford Woodruff Room" in the apostle's honor. It was here that LDS leaders, including Wilford Woodruff, George Q. Cannon, John D. T. McAllister, and others hid from U.S. marshals.

[91] The Fifty-eighth Annual LDS Church Conference was held in Salt Lake City, Apr. 5–6, 1888.

[92] Still in hiding from federal marshals, Woodruff had his general conference address read to the congregation in the tabernacle. For the text of his address, see Wilford Woodruff, "Epistle to the Officers and Members of the Church of Jesus Christ of Latter-day Saints in General Conference Assembled," *Deseret News*, Apr. 11, 1888, 201, 204.

[93] The "underground" was a term used to describe life in hiding from the U.S. marshals searching for polygamist Latter-day Saints.

Salt Lake City, Utah
April 23, 1888

Elder William Atkin
Bloomington, Washington County

Dear Brother

I have laying before me your letter of April 8th, in which you give an account of the visitation of the marshals at St. George and a list of those arrested. You also speak of the fine appearance of the country around you, and of your time of fishing, with Brothers [John] McAllister, [David] Cannon, [William] Thompson etc.

I have also your letter of April 16th, in which you speak of the sickness of Sister [Rachel Thompson] Atkin and the condition of William [Atkin, Jr.]. I hope they will both soon be well again. You speak of the visitation of Brothers McAllister and Cannon and others at your stone room. I am very glad they have a place of retreat there, and that you have a disposition to receive them and treat them kindly, etc. For all this you shall not lose your reward.

I shall give you a call whenever I come into that country. I do not forget the many pleasant hours I have spent there with you. My family are generally well at present. Our trees are only just in bloom in this country; but the whole earth looks as though it was drying up for the want of water. Brother George Q [Cannon] wishes to be remembered to you. Remember us to your family.

Your brother in the gospel
Wilford Woodruff

Salt Lake City, Utah
April 28, 1888

Dear Brother Atkin

I have no time to write a letter today only to say I have enclosed a photo to you today which I hope you will get to see what an old man looks like. We are still in the whirlpool. I don't know how we will come out but trust to the Lord. My love to all the family.

As ever
L[ewis] Allen

Salt Lake City, Utah
May 23, 1888

William Atkin

Dear Brother

Your letter of May 8th is before me. I was pleased to hear from you and to hear that Sister [Rachel Thompson] Atkin had got well again and that William [Atkin, Jr.,] had the board out of his side and that his ribs were better. I hope he will get well. I went to Manti[94] to assist in the dedication of the temple[95] and to organize the company. I did not stop to the public dedication but organized the company. Appointed D[aniel] H Wells to

[94] Manti is a city in Sanpete County, in central Utah. Settled by Isaac Morley and other Mormon pioneers in 1849, it was named after a Book of Mormon city. Van Cott, *Utah Place Names*, 243–44.

[95] The Manti Temple, constructed between 1877 and 1888, was the third LDS House of the Lord finished in Utah. Wilford Woodruff privately offered the dedicatory prayer on May 17, 1888. Elder Lorenzo Snow repeated Woodruff's dedicatory prayer during sessions held days later. Garr et al., *Encyclopedia*, 705.

preside. I met with [John] McAllister, [James] Bleak,[96] [Moses] Farnsworth,[97] and many others. We traveled in the night 40 miles in a carriage to Manti. Came near being turned over 100 feet down the mountain by the teamster getting out of the road but did barely escape. The Manti Temple is the most beautiful building we have ever built. Cost over $1,000,000—[it] ought to be good. I see from the papers they are having a glorious time in the temple as you will see by the [Deseret] News.[98] We are having a great time with [Frank] Dyer the receiver. He is really out after all the property the church has ever owned since we came here. He wants all the temples, [the] tabernacle, and all [that] the Saints own. We hardly know where he will stop. Remember me to all your family and do not stop writing. Men waiting for me on every side. God bless you and all with you.

L[ewis] Allen

Salt Lake City, Utah
June 11, 1888

Brother and Sister Atkin

Dear friends

Your interesting letter of the 5th is before me and I take 4 minutes to answer. G[eorge] Q [Cannon] is with me, and

---

[96] James Godson Bleak (1829–1918), clerk and historian of the LDS Southern Utah Mission, 1861–1901: b. Nov. 15, 1829, in Southwark, England, to Thomas Nelson Bleak and Mary Godson; m. Elizabeth Moore Oct. 14, 1849, in Bethel Green, England; d. Jan. 30, 1918, in St. George. LDS Ancestral File.

[97] Moses Franklin Farnsworth (1834–1906), chief recorder in the LDS Manti Temple, 1888–1906: b. Feb. 5, 1834, in Edinburgh, Ind., to Reuben Farnsworth and Lucinda Kent; m. Elizabeth Jane Stewart Feb. 26, 1857, in Salt Lake City; d. Feb. 25, 1906, in Manti. Jenson, *Biographical Encyclopedia*, 1:522–23; LDS Ancestral File.

[98] See "At Manti," *Deseret News*, May 23, 1888, 293.

Brother Mack[99] J[oseph] F S[mith] is in the city from Washington. We shall be together all night. All is as well as usual with me and family. [Frank] Dyer is still anxious to get some more property from the Lord; somehow he considers himself the Lord's receiver. He has got some half a dozen men [as] deputies loose in the city to see who they can catch so we have to be awake. I hope Sister Atkin is better with her head. I have not seen Brother [Thomas] Bailey[100] since he drove us over the mountains. He did not intend any harm but he did not seem as well acquainted with the road as he ought to have been. We were very fortunate to escape as well as we did. Our weight on the upper side is what kept us from going over. I was sorry to hear of the sentence[101] of [such] men as [William] Carter,[102] [Walter] Granger,[103] and [Warren] Hardy.[104] Put in the mildest [words] you can, we have to say the devil is in such judges and they will go to prison and to hell when their time comes and it

---

[99] "Mack" was apparently a code name for Joseph F. Smith, his grandmother's maiden name.

[100] Likely Thomas Bailey (1869–1942), bishop of the LDS Nephi Ward, Juab Stake: b. Nov. 7, 1869, in Nephi to Langley A. Bailey and Sarah Andrews; m. Mary E. Chapman May 31, 1900, in Manti; d. Feb. 19, 1942, in Salt Lake City. Jenson, *Biographical Encyclopedia*, 3:303; LDS Ancestral File.

[101] On June 1, 1888, Judge Jacob S. Boreman of Utah's Second District Court sentenced Latter-day Saints William Carter, Warren Hardy, Walter Granger, Casper Bryner, Jacob Bastian, and Mark Burgess to six months' jail time and a $300 fine for unlawful cohabitation. Jenson, *Church Chronology*, 162.

[102] William Carter (1821–95), construction worker on the St. George Temple: b. Feb. 12, 1821, in Leadbury, England, to Thomas Carter and Sarah Parker; m. Ellen Benbow Dec. 5, 1843, in Nauvoo, Ill.; d. June 22, 1895, in St. George. Jenson, *Biographical Encyclopedia*, 4:695–96; LDS Ancestral File.

[103] Walter Granger (1821–1904), bishop of the LDS St. George Second and Third Wards, St. George Stake: b. Aug. 4, 1821, in Edinburgh, Scotland, to Robert Granger and Catherine McDonald; m. Catherine Guthrie Mar. 11, 1841, in Paisley, Scotland; d. May 6, 1904, in Cedar City, Utah. Jenson, *Biographical Encyclopedia*, 3:384–85; LDS Ancestral File.

[104] Warren Hardy (1840–93), construction worker on the St. George Temple: b. Sep. 3, 1840, in Bradford, Mass., to Josiah Guile Hardy and Sarah Clark Parker; m. Caroline Lucy Blake Mar. 5, 1864, in Salt Lake City; d. Nov. 22, 1893, in St. George. LDS Ancestral File.

won't be for 6 months but at least 1,000 years. We shall soon have a change of some of the judges and hope of all [improvement]. I have no fear of [them] getting worse. I was also glad to learn of the testimonies in the dedication of the temple. I should think near half of the congregation heard the music and quite a number saw a halo of light surround a number of speakers.[105] There was about 30 with me when I offered the dedicatory prayer upon the altar. I felt the power of God while doing it and would have liked to have been at the public dedication but did not think it wisdom. Emma [Smoot Smith Woodruff] sends love to all [and] so does Alice [Woodruff]. Give my love to all the family. I would like to see all the family once more and have a good time with May [Atkin] and Nellie [Atkin]. I often think of my good times with them. Asahel [Woodruff] has gone up Big Cottonwood [Canyon][106] 4 miles above the paper mill and fenced in about 10 acres in a flat spot [on the] north side of the creek at the head of the stairs and planted the America's flag 1,000 feet high on top of the peaks west of his camp. [He] has put up a lumber pillars and back room and 14 tents, a bowery, a large dining room tent, and commenced to keep a hotel there to accommodate excursionists. This is in connection with the Valley House.[107] A great many are wanting to go there. Good fishing in the Cottonwood, that river by the campground. Asahel thinks they will do well at it. Time must determine it. G[eorge] Q [Cannon] wishes to be remembered. We are all as well as usual. I hope William [Atkin, Jr.,] has better of his fall.

---

[105] See "Spiritual Manifestations in the Manti Temple," *Latter-day Saints' Millennial Star* (England) 33 (Aug. 13, 1888): 520–24.

[106] Big Cottonwood Canyon is in the Wasatch Mountains east of the Salt Lake valley, the easternmost town being Brighton. It was named by Brigham Young after the cottonwood trees that grow near its mouth in abundance. Van Cott, *Utah Place Names*, 31–32.

[107] The Valley House was Woodruff's downtown Salt Lake City home, located on South Temple at about the present-day location of Abravanel Hall.

We have had quite cold weather. It is getting warm now. We are cutting our first lucerne.[108]

I remain as ever your brother
Lewis Allen

Salt Lake City, Utah
July 26, 1888

Brother and Sister Atkin

Dear friends

I received William['s] very interesting letter of June 24th and read it with much interest. And as I have told you before I can only steal a few moments to scribble off a few lines in answer. If I did not do this myself many of my letters would go unanswered for it is all the reporters and clerks can do to answer my public letters. Well what can I say to you? I have finally got off [George] Peters[109] and [Frank] Dyer and [Franklin Snyder] Richards,[110] our lawyer, all off to Washington to see the attorney general and see if we can settle up our affairs. The assistant attorney, [George] Jenks,[111] is the man we are dealing with. He says he will do all he [can] for a settlement. He will throw out all our temples, tabernacle, and meeting houses and not count

---

[108] Lucerne is another name for alfalfa.

[109] Non-Mormon lawyer George S. Peters of Ohio replaced William H. Dickson as Utah's district attorney in April 1887. Jenson, *Church Chronology*, 147.

[110] Franklin Snyder Richards (1849–1934), general counsel for the LDS Church: b. June 20, 1849, in Salt Lake City to Franklin Dewey Richards and Jane Snyder; m. Emily Sophia Tanner Dec. 18, 1868, in Salt Lake City; d. Sep. 4, 1934, in Salt Lake City. Jenson, *Biographical Encyclopedia*, 4:55–59; Garr et al., *Encyclopedia*, 1021–22; LDS Ancestral File.

[111] George Augustus Jenks (1836–1908), solicitor general of the United States, 1886–89: b. Mar. 26, 1836, in Punxsutawney, Penn.; d. Feb. 10, 1908, in Brookville, Penn. *Biographical Directory of the United States Congress*, www.bioguide.congress.gov (hereafter cited as *Biographical Directory of Congress*).

them in at all, for they should be free, and he will have what we
have turned over go up to the Supreme Court to decide upon.
And if they declare the law constitutional I suppose the government will dispose of the property in some way but if the law
is declared unconstitutional the property is to be returned to
us. But a great many gentiles[112] through the whole county say
it is a damn shame for the government to rob us of our hard
earned property so we all say well the 24 is passed and the first
time in my history that I did not attend the celebrations[113] in
person when I was in this part of the county. But I wrote a
short address which was read to the congregation.[114] My health
is as good as can be expected considering the constant amount
of labor that is upon me. Asahel [Woodruff] has gone up Big
Cottonwood [Canyon] 4 miles above the mouth and paper mill
and entered a piece of land as mineral land. On the flat, [he]
cleared off the brush and pitched 15 tents, brought out the water
in different channels and prepared to entertain excursionists
and charges at $1.50 a day or $8 a week. He has had so many
he could not lodge them or feed them, only by setting 2 or 3
tables. I was there 3 days. It is splendid fishing in the creek.
We caught about a 100 while there. I had Emma [Smoot Smith
Woodruff] and Alice [Woodruff] with me. I go again Saturday night to spend about a week with Emma, Clara [Wood-
ruff Beebe], Blanch [Woodruff],[115] Alice [Woodruff], Ovando

---

[112] "Gentile" was a term that Latter-day Saints (and even members of other faiths) used to describe
non-Mormons, in addition to referring to non-Jews. Garr et al., *Encyclopedia*, 420–21.

[113] July 24 is celebrated annually as "Pioneer Day" in Utah to commemorate the 1847 arrival
of the vanguard Mormon pioneer company's arrival in the Salt Lake valley. Garr et al.,
Encyclopedia, 921–22.

[114] For the text of Woodruff's address, see "Pioneer Day," *Deseret News*, Aug. 1, 1888, 462.

[115] Winnifred Blanch Woodruff (1876–1954), a daughter of Wilford Woodruff and Emma
Smoot Smith: b. Apr. 9, 1876, in Salt Lake City; m. Joseph John, Jr., Daynes Dec. 18, 1895,
in Salt Lake City; d. Apr. 28, 1954, in Salt Lake City. Jackson, *Wilford Woodruff Family*;
LDS Ancestral File.

[Beebe],[116] and Owen [Woodruff] to rest and get away from here and work. Brother G[eorge] Q C[annon] is well and wishes to be remembered. Brother J[oseph] F S[mith] is quite sick in bed with lumbago[117] and sciatica.[118] I go around about the county quite freely without any trouble. And was it not for keeping company with Mack and Addy[119] I expect I could go openly but I hope they will soon be free. We have two new judges appointed and confirmed.[120] I hope they will do better than those removed. Give my love to all the family. What man was that who died at Price[121] a few days since? I suppose you have your harvest all up. We are only just beginning to cut our wheat. I have bored two artesian wells at Emma [Smith Woodruff]'s. I drove one 300 feet for more water but got none, had to drove the pipe up to 125 feet for 12 gallons, bored another 65 feet [and] got 10 gallons. They gave me water enough to water my garden lawn and all the ground as far as 150 feet. Hope will reach on what the water can run. Well I must quit, my 10 minutes are up. God bless you all is my prayer. All my family sends love.

As ever yours
L[ewis] Allen

---

[116] Ovando Collins Beebe (1867–1928), a son-in-law of Wilford Woodruff and Emma Smoot Smith: b. May 14, 1867, in Polk City, Iowa, to George Beebe and Esther Ann Rogers; m. Clara Martina Woodruff Aug. 3, 1887; d. Dec. 27, 1928. Jackson, *Wilford Woodruff Family;* LDS Ancestral File.

[117] Lumbago is terrible pain caused by muscle strain in the lower back.

[118] Sciatica is pain along the sciatic nerve in the lower back, buttocks, and hips.

[119] "Addy" is an unknown code name for a church leader.

[120] In July 1888, President Grover Cleveland nominated Elliott Sandford and John W. Judd as justices of the Utah Territorial Supreme Court. They were both confirmed that same month. Jenson, *Church Chronology,* 163.

[121] Price is a ghost town in Washington County, in southwestern Utah. Settled by Mormon pioneers as Heberville in 1858, its name was changed to Price in 1874; it was abandoned by the turn of the twentieth century. Van Cott, *Utah Place Names,* 303.

Salt Lake City, Utah
August 14, 1888

William Atkin

Dear Brother

I have lying before me [your letters] of July 29th and August 7th both of which I read with much interest. You ask about Asahel [Woodruff]. I took Emma [Woodruff] and Blanch [Woodruff], Alice [Woodruff], Clara [Beebe] & husband Ovando Beebe and went up to Asahel's lodge and spent about a week with him. I took up 2 tents with me and the 2nd night he had so much company he could not accommodate them with tents. I let him have both of mine and went into the [—] with my wife and the children slept the best they could. Asahel had no place to sleep. But he soon got 20 tents pitched and all had a place to sleep. He had about 50 guests but they go and come. He has some 30 now. There has been so many fishermen that they nearly drained the creek near the camp. Ovando and another brag fisherman started up the creek for a day fishing at 7 o'clock. I went up with my carriage at 11 o'clock to find them and fish some. I did not find them but commenced fishing at 1 o'clock and fished 5 hours and caught 20 fine trout and hauled a good many more out of water that I did not get. And before I got into camp I overtook the two fishermen that went out early in the morning and they had 2 little small trout and when we went into camp there was a great hurrah in camp because an old man beat 2 young men so badly in fishing. Asahel and myself beat them all in fishing. He has got a very good place for excursionist[s] in the summer as it is the nearest place from the city. He was hardly prepared for it this season. He has entered the land as mineral land. I think he would do well next season there if he was prepared. G[eorge] Q C[annon] and J[oseph] F S[mith] are both with me now. J F S has just got able to get out but he has to lie down most of the time. Our lawyer F[ranklin] S. Richards has got home from Washington. So has [Frank] Dyer and [George] Peters. I think the two latter are modified since their visit to Washington and [their] interview with assistant attorney [George] Jenks, and the instructions they got. I don't yet know how we will pay our note to Dyer the 1 September for $158,000 but we will have to trust in the Lord for it. H[orace] S. Eldredge['s][122] name with mine and others are on the note. I visited Brother Eldredge yesterday. He is considered by the doctors to be at death's door. He is a very sick man and doctors say he cannot live. I suppose he is the richest man in the church but riches don't keep a man alive. My family are well and my own health is good at present. I have had 3 artesian wells dug on my farm, 2 at Emma['s], one at [Sarah] Delight [Stocking Woodruff]'s.[123] I sunk one well at Emma's—300 feet and no water. Drew my pipe up to 180 feet, got 10 gallons a minute. Drove another 65 feet 75 feet west of the first [and] got 10 gallons a minute. Drove one for Asahel at the S. E. corner of the lot 145 feet [deep] and got 20 gallons a minute. Drove one at Delight's 80 feet [and] got 20 gallons a minute good water. A well in 19 [—] 30 feet [with] 6 inch pipe yields 300 gallons a minute. Emma and all want to be remembered to you all. I am glad Sister [Rachel Thompson] Atkin got better. I hope you will all enjoy good health.

I remain as ever yours
L[ewis] Allen

---

[122] Horace Sunderlin Eldredge (1816–88), one of the LDS First Seven Presidents of the Seventies, 1854–88: b. Feb. 6, 1816, in Brutus, N.Y., to Alanson Eldredge and Esther Sunderlin; m. Betsy Ann Chase July 20, 1836, in Buffalo, N.Y.; d. Sep. 6, 1888, in Salt Lake City. Jenson, *Biographical Encyclopedia*, 1:196–97; LDS Ancestral File.

[123] Sarah Delight Stocking Woodruff (1838–1906), a plural wife of Wilford Woodruff: b. July 26, 1838, in Canton, Conn., to John Jay Stocking and Catharine Emeline Ensign; m. Wilford Woodruff July 31, 1857, in Salt Lake City; d. May 28, 1906, in Big Cottonwood Canyon, Utah. Sarah Delight and Woodruff had seven children: Marion, Emeline, Ensign, Jeremiah, Rosanna, John Jay, and Julia Delight (see appendix 2). Jackson, *Wilford Woodruff Family;* LDS Ancestral File.

Salt Lake City, Utah
September 12, 1888

Brother and Sister Atkin

Dear friends

Your letter of September 2nd is before me and in the midst of a whirlpool of business I will try to write a few lines. I dare not put off answering my correspondence nowadays. If I do it will never be done. I have 3 heavy meetings a day and not much less than a dozen meetings a day of one kind and another and go in very difficult matters to attend to with government officers etc. In fact I have never been in deeper water in my life in church matters than today. Well I call myself well as usual and so with the brethren with me. We hope to see daylight some day before long. I am always glad to hear from you and of your posterity. I have no news except what you get through the press. If I had I have no time to write it. You will see H[orace] S Eldredge is buried and his will published but not very satisfactorily to his first children. We shall hold conference in S[alt] L[ake] City coming on the 5 October. *I may attend but can't say*. Now my young children all go to school. Alice [Woodruff] is beginning to learn. Well now she and her mother are both well. Now Brother Atkin you can see that I am nervous and in a hurry today. I have so many irons in the fire that some of them are burning so excuse [my] haste and [this] short letter. But I will say that [Francis] Daggett[124] is as good a probate judge as you can get outside and they object in the [U.S.] Senate to appointing a Mormon anywhere. Old [George] Edmunds[125]

---

[124] Francis L. Daggett served as a judge in the Washington County (Utah) probate court between October 1888 and October 1892.

[125] George Franklin Edmunds (1828–1919), Republican U.S. senator from Vermont (1866–91), congressional cosponsor of the Edmunds-Tucker Act of 1887: b. Feb. 1, 1828, in Richmond, Vt.; d. Feb. 27, 1919, in Pasadena, Calif. *Biographical Directory of Congress*.

is the chairman of the committee in the Senate who confirmed. He will object to a Mormon. Give my love to all the family.

As ever yours
Lewis Allen

Salt Lake City, Utah
October 24, 1888

Dear Brother and Sister Atkin

I received your kind letter of the 7th, and read with interest as I do all your letters. I was sorry to learn of Sister Atkin's sickness. I hope she will soon be well again. Well we have finally got our cause through the Utah supreme court and the appeal [has] gone up to the U.S. Supreme Court so it gives me a little rest upon that point for a while. I don't know what the U.S. court will do with it. I have been spending a week on the shore of Utah Lake at Brother Madsen's[126] to get away from business. 4 of us in company, we caught in all about 100 lbs. of trout in nets and 150 ducks. I did not kill any ducks as I would not wade through mud and water after them as the others did. I have got back to my post again but as full of business as ever; [I] was up on Monday night in council until 1 o'clock. The judge has decided against us in Idaho which makes it bad for the people there.[127]

---

[126] Likely Peter Madsen (1824–1910), bishop of the LDS Provo 5th Ward, Utah Stake, 1877–92: b. Apr. 6, 1824, in Studsdal, Denmark, to Mads Peterson Madsen and Mette Marie Madsen; m. Caroline Jensen Apr. 25, 1860, in Utah; d. Aug. 20, 1911, in Provo, Utah. Jenson, *Biographical Encyclopedia*, 4:614; LDS Ancestral File; LDS Family Search International Genealogical Index, database available at www.familysearch.org.

[127] In 1884, the Idaho territorial legislature passed the Idaho Test Oath, which barred anyone who "engaged in or belonged to an organization that advocated" plural marriage from voting. This anti-Mormon legislation prevented Latter-day Saints living in Idaho from being part of the political and judicial process. This decision essentially rendered the First Amendment free-exercise clause meaningless, as it allowed Idaho to disfranchise Latter-day Saints for their beliefs, not just for their actions. In October 1888, Judge C. H. Berry upheld the legislation. Jenson, *Church Chronology*, 166; personal correspondence, Thomas G. Alexander.

G[eorge] Q C[annon] enjoys himself as well as any man in the pen [penitentiary].[128] Has all the privileges he wants, eats ducks, and sleeps well. I write him often. I am glad your sheep are doing well. I don't know whether they miss me about sweeping their fleeces or not.[129] I would like to be with you in your fishing excursions and help catch a few. You must excuse my short letters. Give my love to all the family not forgetting the boys and girls. Alice [Woodruff] is going to school. They all would send love if they knew I was writing.

I remain as ever your brother
L[ewis] Allen

⌒⌒

Salt Lake City, Utah
November 2, 1888

William Atkin

Dear Brother

Your letter of October 25th is before me and its contents noted with care and in reply [I] will say that I have no special trouble with those directly connected with me. Of course we have a variety of opinion upon busy subjects. Some of the deep water spoken of was [that Frank] Dyer and [George] Peters wrote us to do away with polygamy in our settlement with the government. I told our 5 lawyers including Broadbent and Sheets and Rawlins I would see the whole nation *damned first*. Another trouble was the state of our brethren in Idaho. I have *worried over them*. There are hundreds of them who have taken the oath,

---

[128] After years of life on the underground, George Q. Cannon finally yielded to U.S. marshals, who arrested him for practicing plural marriage (he had five wives and thirty-two children). Cannon was incarcerated for six months in the Utah Territorial Penitentiary until his release on Feb. 21, 1889. Powell, *Utah History Encyclopedia*, 71; Jenson, *Church Chronology*, 171.

[129] When Woodruff was hiding with the Atkins, he helped them shear their sheep.

registered [to vote], and even withdrawn from the church for the purpose of voting. And they are all liable to be convicted of perjury but the governor has promised to pardon them all, that is the condition they are in today. It has caused me a great deal of anxiety but I hope for the best. I am still overworked with care and business from 25 to 75 letters a day to be read and answered and upon every subject imaginable. George Q [Cannon] is enjoying himself in the pen very well. Is quite busy. Has a good deal of freedom for a prisoner. My health is still good except [for a] severe cold. (I would like you to burn this letter or take care of it.) Give my love to all the family. I hope Sister [Rachel Thompson] Atkin will keep well.

As ever yours
L[e]wis A[llen]

Salt Lake City, Utah
November 23, 1888

Brother and Sister Atkin

I received Brother William [Atkin's] letter of the 12th and as I am devoting an hour or so to catch up my correspondence I will write a few lines to you. I think I made a mistake in my last letter in speaking of my duck hunt. I intended to say I did *not think it* my duty to wade through mud and water for ducks. I don't know what words I used but no matter. I was glad to hear that you was well and especially to know that Sister [Rachel Thompson] Atkin was well, for when there is but one woman to near a dozen men she ought to have very good health in order to wait upon so many men. My health is about as usual but still [feeling] some [of my] cold but as full of business as ever

and still some of it *unpleasant*. We have not got through dealing with men who are still after the spoils. I am dealing with
the most hungry lot of men for the spoils I ever had in hand
and all things do not go smooth. G[eorge] Q [Cannon] is still
well in the pen and feels pretty well only he does not like to see
so many coming in flocks. Of course the ring and Republicans
now expect to take the kingdom. If they do, it will be a different
kingdom from ours but I think both political parties can dwell
in the same kingdom for there is no difference that I see. Excuse
this short letter. Give my love to all the family.

As ever yours
L[ewis] Allen

Salt Lake City, Utah
December 12, 1888

William Atkin

Dear Brother
   Your letter of the 1st is before me. I have read it carefully I
will say in relation to the sheep I have talked with [William]
Preston[130] upon the subject. He informs me he has made the
arrangements to give credit as you desired.[131] About the change
of the presidency in St. George. We are releasing all the presidents of temples from presiding over the stakes.[132] It is very

---

[130] William Bowker Preston (1830–1908), presiding bishop of the LDS Church, 1884–1907: b.
    Nov. 24, 1830, in Halifax, Va., to Christopher Preston and Martha Mitchell Clayton; m.
    Harriet A. Thatcher Feb. 24, 1858, in Salt Lake City; d. Aug. 2, 1908, in Salt Lake City.
    Jenson, *Biographical Encyclopedia*, 1:232–35, 3:771; LDS Ancestral File.
[131] William Atkin had likely asked for tithing credit for something he donated to the LDS
    Church. As the presiding bishop, William Preston had discretion over these financial
    matters.
[132] A stake is an LDS administrative ecclesiastical unit comprising several local congregations,
    similar to a Catholic diocese.

necessary to separate the two, for good reasons. I hope Brother [Daniel] McArthur[133] will do well. I cannot tell about this [changing of] councilors until it is tried. Well [Charles] Zane undertook to break up [Frank] Dyer and settlement with the church. He thought Dyer had not got property enough. But Zane got mashed in the matter and quit. He had more *scoundrel lawyers* to fight than he could stand. I don't know what will come next. Our cause has been advanced on the calendar in the Supreme Court and January will decide our case one way or the other.[134] I am in fair health. My cold still lingers on. Joseph F S[mith] and [John] Nuttall are with me and are quite well. We are having altogether too fine weather. If we do not get some snow in the mountains this winter we may look for a famine in the near future. Give my love to Sister [Rachel Thompson] Atkin and all the family not forgetting the girls. I expect John W. Taylor[135] and perhaps John Henry Smith[136] at conference.

I remain as ever yours
L[ewis] Allen

[133] Daniel Duncan McArthur (1820–1908), president of the LDS St. George Stake, 1888–1901: b. Apr. 8, 1820, in Holland, N.Y., to Duncan McArthur and Susan McKeen; m. Matilda Caroline Fuller Dec. 14, 1845, in Nauvoo, Ill.; d. June 3, 1908, in St. George. Jenson, *Biographical Encyclopedia*, 1:336–37; LDS Ancestral File.

[134] The U.S. Supreme Court would issue its ruling on *The Late Corporation of the Mormon Church v. United States* in May 1890.

[135] John Whittaker Taylor (1858–1916), member of the LDS Quorum of the Twelve Apostles, 1884–1905: b. May 15, 1858, in Provo, Utah, to John Taylor and Sophia Whittaker; m. May Leona Rich Oct. 18, 1882, in Salt Lake City; d. Oct. 10, 1916, in Salt Lake City. Jenson, *Biographical Encyclopedia*, 1:151–56; Garr et al., *Encyclopedia*, 1226; LDS Ancestral File.

[136] John Henry Smith (1848–1911), member of the LDS Quorum of the Twelve Apostles, 1880–1911: b. Sep. 18, 1848, in Kanesville, Iowa, to George A. Smith and Sarah Ann Libby; m. Sarah Farr Oct. 20, 1866, in Salt Lake City; d. Oct. 13, 1911, in Salt Lake City. Jenson, *Biographical Encyclopedia*, 1:141–44; Garr et al., *Encyclopedia*, 1122; LDS Ancestral File.

LETTERS OF 1889

Salt Lake City, Utah
January 9, 1889

William Atkin

Dear Brother

I always make it a point to steal time enough to answer all the letters you write me. I read your last letter of December 29th to Emma [Smith Woodruff] and she wanted me to say to you that while she has great confidence in your word upon almost every subject yet she says it is hard work for her to comprehend the truth that your 210 lb. doctor did really keep you one day and night in boiling water and red hot salt. She thinks if that were really so that after going through your ordeal you would be so badly cooked that your doctor could always handle you after that but I expect it was true or you would not have said so but there is hardly anything to what limit a Mormon can go through. As to myself I am enjoying fair health. My cold is still with me more or less. I had a very poor time 2 weeks ago. Was in council with the Twelve [Apostles] till midnight. Was taken while in meeting with something like the vertigo or blind staggers. I could not walk straight or hardly at all. It lasted about 24 hours before I got over it but I came all right again. Asahel [Woodruff] has sold out his affair in the Valley House. I was very glad to have him get out for we found out that he got with the wrong men to do business with. We will lose his summer work and about $600 and glad to get off so Asahel sold out to Mr. Carter, a stockman. I hardly know how our affairs will go in Washington for a state government. It does not look very favorable. Give my love to Sister [Rachel Thompson] Atkin and all the family.

Your brother
L[ewis] Allen

Salt Lake City, Utah
January 30, 1889

William Atkin

Dear Brother

Your letter of the 20th is before me so I will answer it. At least I will write you in return. We had a serious accident here last night on John W. Young's[137] railroad.[138] You will see the account in the Herald.[139] The rails were covered with ice and snow and the brakes would not work and they went down the mountain with lightning speed and with 8 cars loaded with stone and as the cars were about to leave the track the 6 men on board jumped off and Joseph A. Young[140] (Joseph A.['s][141] son) and George Walker[142] were instantly killed. [J. W.] McDonald and [Charles] McCarty were severely injured; the two later were buried under the wreck but not fatally injured. It is the first

---

[137] John Willard Young (1844–1924), apostle and counselor in the LDS First Presidency: b. Oct. 1, 1844, in Nauvoo, Ill., to Brigham Young and Mary Ann Angell; m. Lucy Maria Canfield Feb. 16, 1864, in Salt Lake City; d. Feb. 11, 1924, in New York City. Jenson, *Biographical Encyclopedia,* 1:42; Garr et al., *Encyclopedia,* 1380–81; LDS Ancestral File.

[138] The Red Butte branch of the Salt Lake and Fort Douglas Railway.

[139] For accounts of this tragedy, see "Killed in Red Butte," *Salt Lake Herald,* Jan. 30, 1889; and "Two Railway Men Slain," *Salt Lake Tribune,* Jan. 30, 1889.

[140] Joseph Angell Young, Jr. (1868–89): b. Nov. 8, 1868, in Salt Lake City, to Joseph Angell Young and Mary Ann J. Ayers; d. Jan. 29, 1889, in Salt Lake City. LDS Pedigree Research File; LDS International Genealogical Index.

[141] Joseph Angell Young (1834–75), first president of the LDS Sevier Stake: b. Oct. 14, 1834, in Kirtland, Ohio, to Brigham Young and Mary Ann Angell; m. Clara Federata Stenhouse Mar. 4, 1867, in Salt Lake City; d. Aug. 5, 1875, in Manti, Utah. Jenson, *Biographical Encyclopedia,* 1:518–19; LDS Ancestral File.

[142] George Walker was a man in his early twenties living in the Sugar House Ward, Salt Lake City.

accident on that train. Our brethren will soon come home from Washington. We will have no state government this session. We do not yet know whether the Supreme Court will decide to take our property or not—time must determine. My health is pretty good now, still [have] some [of my] cold. I expect Brother G[eorge] Q [Cannon] with me in about 2 weeks. F[rancis] M. Lyman[143] has a brother joining him. They were both well. My family are all well as usual. Asahel [Woodruff] has got his old place in the Co-op[144] and feels at home again. I am as busy as ever. No slack up in work. Give my love to all your family. I don't think the ducks or fish in your pond are looking for any more trouble from me. Yet I would like to look at them some more.

> I remain as ever your brother
> L[ewis] Allen

Salt Lake City, Utah
March 18, 1889

William Atkin
Bloomington, Washington County

Dear Brother William

Your letter of February 4th came duly to hand. Press of other matters have prevented me from answering sooner. Since then,

---

[143] Francis Marion Lyman (1840–1916), member of the LDS Quorum of the Twelve Apostles, 1880–1916: b. Jan. 12, 1840, in Good Hope, Ill., to Amasa M. Lyman and Maria Louisa Tanner; m. Rhoda Ann Taylor Nov. 18, 1857, in San Bernardino, Calif.; d. Nov. 18, 1916 in Salt Lake City. Jenson, *Biographical Encyclopedia*, 1:136–41; Garr et al., *Encyclopedia*, 687; LDS Ancestral File.

[144] Zion's Cooperative Mercantile Institution (ZCMI), founded in 1868, was a chain of LDS Church–owned department stores headquartered in Salt Lake City until it was divested in 1999. Asahel was an officer of the corporation for many years. Garr et al., *Encyclopedia*, 1394–95.

as you are aware, Brother G[eorge] Q [Cannon] has regained his liberty, and is greatly enjoying it and improving it by visiting and meeting with the Saints whenever opportunity permits. On his first sentence he received no benefit of the "Copper Act,"[145] as it is called, because the term of imprisonment was shorter than law contemplated for such benefits. But under the second sentence—100 days—he got the full benefit allowed by the "Copper Act"—that is, five days off per month, or about fifteen days.

In regard to getting a state government for Utah, I cannot see but it will be just as consistent for the Lord to soften the hearts of the "powers that be" to give the people of Utah their right, in some small degree, in the form of a state government, as to soften them to administer the harsh laws they have made to rule us by, in some degree of mildness and humanity. We are now, politically speaking, a dependency or ward of the United States; but in a state capacity we would be freed from such dependency, and would possess the powers and independence of a sovereign state, with authority to make and execute our own laws. And being such, we would, in the event of the disruption of the general government, be independent of all earthly powers and clothed with legal as well as divine authority to assume the position in the earth God has designed or may design us to fill in such an event. As statehood seems to promise the readiest solution for some of the prominent questions involved in the great problem of the hour, and no other way has as yet been manifested, it would seem proper for us to bend our faith and energies in that direction, that, if it should prove to be the will of the Lord, we may be found striving for that object; and should it not prove to be the will of the Lord for us to get a state government, then would we be justified in that we acted according to the

---

[145] The Copper Act of 1880 allowed for the shortening of prison sentences of inmates for good behavior. Larson, *Prisoner for Polygamy*, 95.

best light and wisdom we possessed. And in conclusion upon this point, I may add that if it be the will of the Lord that Utah should become a state, "all hell will be powerless to hinder it," just as you say; and certainly we should be found in that accord with God's will. It is proper that we should strive to accomplish his purposes, always acting upon the best light we possess.

I am glad to hear that little Nellie [Atkin] was preserved though her sore affliction and was spared. To God be ascribed the honor, though the services of Dr. [Silas] Higgins[146] were had.

Wilford [Woodruff, Jr.,] is living in the city, has quit farming, and is now engaged delivering goods for zcmi.

The visitation of such a heavy snow storm, at the season of year you wrote, is rather an unusual occurrence for "Dixie,"[147] but none the less welcome to the farmer and owner of stock. Our winter has been open and dry. We are threatened with another dry season, which will be serious for the farmers, as the two or three past seasons have also been very dry. We have just had some very nice gentle rains, which have moistened the ground and will be a great help to plowing and seeding.

It looks now, in view of the constantly increasing labors devolving upon me, as though I would not get an opportunity very soon of again disturbing the fish and game of the pond, as in days past; but in that regard my inability or disappointment will be their pleasure, no doubt.

Doubtless, the decision of the Supreme Court, for which we are looking hourly, will be a "mixture of good and bad." But we shall rejoice if any good shall come to *us* by their politico-

---

[146] Silas Gardner Higgins (1822–1904), southern Utah pioneer physician: b. Nov. 16, 1822, in Gray, Maine, to George Higgins and Lydia Young; m. Nancy Louisa Clark June 19, 1859, in Ogden, Utah; d. Aug. 18, 1904, in St. George. Andrew Karl Larson, *The Red Hills of November: A Pioneer Biography of Utah's Cotton Town* (Salt Lake City: Deseret News Press, 1959), 274; lds Ancestral File.

[147] "Dixie" was a term used to describe the lds Southern Utah Mission, as Brigham Young attempted to grow cotton in the milder climate.

judicial Nazareth. We will thank the Lord for any *right* that may be vouchsafed to us, and for all favors we will praise Him, as in duty bound we should "acknowledge His hand in all things."

My family are usually well, and I am recovering from a severe cold contracted by over-exertion and improper ventilation during my recent visit to Utah County, where Brother [George] Cannon and I attended twelve meetings in three days. I had never visited any part of Utah where there seemed more need of preaching the good word than in Utah County. After four years or more of comparative seclusion, Brother Cannon and I had a feeling akin to that of young elders and boys starting upon a mission. I enjoyed it very much, with the exception of taking a cold.

With love to all, I am your brother,
Wilford Woodruff

Salt Lake City, Utah
May 3, 1889

William Atkin
Bloomington, Washington County

Dear Brother

I received your letter of April 8th, but have never had a moment that I could answer it until now.

Brother George Q. [Cannon] and myself enjoy our freedom very much. We held 12 meetings in three days in Utah County, and I had a very interesting conference on Sunday and Monday last at Brigham City.[148] About two thousand of the inhabitants

---

[148] Brigham City is a city in Box Elder County, in northwestern Utah. Settled as Box Elder and then Youngsville by Mormon pioneers in 1850, its name was changed to Brigham City in 1867 in honor of Brigham Young, second president of the LDS Church. Van Cott, *Utah Place Names*, 50.

met us at the depot on our arrival on Sunday, and we had much of the spirit of teaching and instruction in our meetings. I start in the morning for Logan, to attend the conference there on Sunday and Monday. Brother George Q. and myself have recently returned from a mission to California, where we spent ten days and had a great deal [of business] and [met] a great many people, and traveled considerably in the state. We went to Monterey[149] and north of the geysers.[150] We were satisfied from our observation of men and things that the Lord is at work for us, although, of course, the devil is against us.

We had quite a celebration[151] here on Tuesday, April 30th, the same as was held, I suppose, throughout the United States. You will see the oration and speeches and proceedings in the Deseret News.[152]

Business increases upon me almost daily, until I sometimes hardly know how to wade through it. I am glad to hear of your prosperity, and that your family and sheep are doing well, and that another of your sons is married.[153] I expect everything looks forward and flourishing with you. We are having a very early spring, but a very dry time: scarcely any snow in the mountains. It is the driest season probably we have ever had. Unless we have rain, the crops will fail in a great measure. We have no officers yet appointed for Utah. I am in hopes that when they are appointed they will be from outside of the Territory, which I rather think will be the case.

---

[149] Monterey is a city in Monterey County, in western California, that was settled by Catholic Franciscan missionaries in 1770.

[150] Woodruff is referring to Old Faithful Geyser in Calistoga, California, which is named after its famous counterpart in Yellowstone National Park.

[151] April 30, 1889, marked the one-hundredth anniversary of the inauguration of U.S. president George Washington.

[152] See "The Celebration," *Deseret News,* May 4, 1889, 590–97.

[153] John Peter Atkin (1867–94) married Annie Walker, a daughter of Charles Lowell Walker and Abigail Middlemass, on February 28, 1889, in St. George, Utah. Awerkamp, *Journal and Genealogies;* LDS Ancestral File.

You must excuse short letters from me these days. Give my love to your wife and to your sons and daughters. Emma [Smith Woodruff] wishes to be remembered to you and family.

As ever, your brother
W[ilford] Woodruff

Salt Lake City, Utah
May 29, 1889

Elder William Atkin

Dear Brother

Your letter of May 20th is before me. I make it a point to answer all letters as far as I can as they come before me. My health is about as usual, except a severe cold that for a day or two deprived me of my speech. Brother George Q. Cannon and myself have been attending conference of late. We went through Sanpete,[154] attended the conference, and held nine meetings, and one at Nephi. We had full houses, and much interest was manifested. The sectarians, priest and people attended some of our meetings. We attended the tabernacle in this city last Sunday. Brother George Q. Cannon spoke and occupied the time, as I was too hoarse to speak at all. All our crops are quite forward. We have had some fine rains: but it is getting dry again. They are beginning to cut the first crop of lucerne. Concerning the government I can only say that [Benjamin] Harrison[155] is showing his hand by appointing such men as [Arthur] Thomas[156] for

---

[154] Sanpete County is a region in central Utah named after San Pitch, the Ute chief whose tribe lived in the area. Van Cott, *Utah Place Names,* 330.

[155] Benjamin Harrison (1833–1901), twenty-third president of the United States, 1889–93; Republican senator from Indiana, 1881–87: b. Aug. 20, 1833, in North Bend, Ohio; d. Mar. 13, 1901, in Indianapolis, Ind. *Biographical Directory of Congress.*

[156] Arthur Lloyd Thomas (1851–1924), governor of Utah, 1889–93: b. Aug. 22, 1851, in Chicago; m. Helena Reinberg; d. Sep. 15, 1924, in Salt Lake City. Powell, *Utah History Encyclopedia,* 550.

governor and [Charles] Zane for chief justice; and it seems as though he intended to make a clean sweep of all Democrats and put Republicans in their place. I do not look for much peace in Utah during his reign. The "ring"[157] intends to steal S[alt] L[ake] City at the next election;[158] but it rather looks as though they won't be able to do it. My family are generally well. Remember me kindly to all your family. Emma [Smith Woodruff] and Alice [Woodruff] wish to be remembered to you.

As ever, your brother
W[ilford] Woodruff

Salt Lake City, Utah
July 5, 1889

Elder William Atkin

Dear Brother

Your letter of June 22nd is before me. I have read it with interest. I am always pleased to hear from you and your family. I hope you may enjoy health and the blessings of life.

Concerning myself, I have had some quite poor turns of late, but I am in the enjoyment of fair health at present, though as busy as ever. Yesterday we kept the 4th of July by going up to Wasatch, in Little Cottonwood Canyon,[159] the place where

---

[157] "The ring" was a term that Latter-day Saints used to describe the non-Mormon Republican political opposition in Utah. The Mormons borrowed this term from charges made during the presidential administration of Ulysses S. Grant, of those groups that were cheating the federal government and their fellow citizens. Personal correspondence with Thomas G. Alexander.

[158] This election was a watershed in Mormon-gentile relations, as the gentiles controlled the Salt Lake City government for the first time. Personal correspondence with Thomas G. Alexander.

[159] Little Cottonwood Canyon is in the Wasatch Mountains east of the Salt Lake valley, the easternmost town being Alta. It was named after the cottonwood trees that grow near its mouth in abundance. Van Cott, *Utah Place Names*, 228.

we have quarried and are quarrying the rock for our temple.[160] Our brethren have built quite a little village there, composed of tents and small cabins, and planted very nice flower gardens and walks, and brought the water through the village. We had a very interesting day. There were about three hundred persons present. We had speeches and various entertainments, and a fete. We visited the stone quarry, which I was deeply interested in. Rocks twice the size of your house are being split up into blocks of the finest granite in the world. I was very much surprised to see their manner of operation. They drill holes in the side of a rock fifty feet high and drive in little wedges which split it straight open, and they then cut it up into blocks.

I am glad that you are doing so well in your grain harvest. We are having a very dry time—the driest ever known in this part of Utah. Many of the crops will not mature. We are approaching our harvest in this country. We have a great many visitors in Utah from the East—congressmen and others. I have a great many callers, wishing interviews with me upon various subjects. We have a meeting today of the Twelve [Apostles] and the presidents of stakes. Our enemies have great hopes of stealing our city and territory. How much they will accomplish, time must determine. We shall do the best we can, trusting in God. In consequence of this meeting, I must make this letter short.

Give my love to your family and to enquiring friends. Emma [Woodruff] and all wish to be remembered to you.

Your brother in the gospel
W[ilford] Woodruff

---

[160] The LDS Salt Lake Temple was constructed over a period of forty years (1853–93) in downtown Salt Lake City from massive granite blocks quarried from the mouth of Little Cottonwood Canyon. Garr et al., *Encyclopedia*, 1056–57.

Salt Lake City, Utah
August 15, 1889

Elder William Atkin
Atkinville[161]

Dear Brother

I am busy as ever and have not therefore time to write a lengthy letter in reply to your favor of the 28th of July. I was very pleased to hear from you, and that all was well with you. My health at present is quite good. You are very fortunate in having plenty of water in that part of the country. We are still suffering for the want of this necessary element. We have had one or two slight showers of rain lately, but not enough to lay the dust. The weather still continues very hot, and everything almost is burning up. It is said that this is the hottest season ever known in Salt Lake. I see that you also have had a share of it.

Our election passed off quietly. The result shows to us that the People's Party[162] in this city will have to be very wide awake to cast every vote they have in order to save the city at the next election. Our people have been rather careless and indifferent in the past in political matters. Now they have got to arouse themselves and do all in their power to prevent our opponents from gaining the ascendancy.

Brother George Q. Cannon and myself have just returned

---

[161] Atkinville is a ghost town in Washington County, in southwestern Utah. In 1877, the family of William and Rachel Thompson Atkin settled the area on the east bank of the Virgin River, about eight miles southwest of St. George, near Price City and Bloomington. They were later joined by William's brother and sister-in-law, Henry and Selena Atkin, and his sister and brother-in-law, William and Adelaide Laxton. Van Cott, *Utah Place Names*, 15; Reid L. Neilson, *From the Green Hills of England to the Red Hills of Dixie: The Story of William and Rachel Thompson Atkin* (Provo, Utah: Red Rock Publishing, 2000), 85–95.

[162] During the late nineteenth century, the People's Party was the political party in Utah affiliated with the LDS Church (in opposition to the non-Mormon Liberal Party) and was supported by the church newspaper, the *Deseret News*. Powell, *Utah History Encyclopedia*, 133.

from a trip to Bear Lake Stake.[163] We held conference there with the people, and had a very enjoyable time. The people of that stake have just erected a very fine tabernacle—about the best in the Territory, outside of Salt Lake. We have also attended conferences recently at Logan, Grantsville,[164] and Ogden. We had excellent meetings at each place, and a good spirit prevailed.

With kind regards to yourself and wife and family, in which Brothers George Q. Cannon and Joseph F. Smith join, and praying the Lord to bless you,

I am as ever, your brother
Wilford Woodruff

⟞⟞

Salt Lake City, Utah
October 18, 1889

Elder William Atkin

Dear Brother

Your letter of September 29th has been received, but I have had no chance to answer it until now. We are still overwhelmed with business almost day and night. I went south and spent three days at Deseret, and have returned. We are having meetings almost constantly on our city affairs and other matters.

My health is about as usual, and my family are generally well.

---

[163] The LDS Bear Lake Stake, founded in 1869, was an administrative ecclesiastical unit comprising several local congregations, encompassing Latter-day Saints living in Bear Lake County, Idaho, and northern Rich County, Utah. Andrew Jenson, *Encyclopedic History of the Church of Jesus Christ of Latter-day Saints* (Salt Lake City: Deseret News Publishing Company, 1941), 46–48 (hereafter cited as *Encyclopedic History*).

[164] Grantsville is a city in Toole County in northwestern Utah. Originally called Twenty Wells by the Donner party in 1846, the area was later settled by Mormon pioneers, who renamed it Grantsville, in honor of George D. Grant, who protected the town from American Indians in 1851. Van Cott, *Utah Place Names*, 162–63.

I am glad to hear that all is well with you. I expect to start next Monday for Canada, to be gone three or four weeks.[165]

All send love. Alice [Woodruff] often speaks of you and the family, as does Emma [Smith Woodruff]. All wish to be remembered to you and family. I am glad that you are prospering in your wool business. We are beginning to have some heavy rains, and the weather had become quite cool. I have no time to write long letters today. I feel to say, God bless you and all pertaining to you.

Your brother,
W[ilford] Woodruff

Salt Lake City, Utah
December 12, 1889

William Atkin

Dear Brother

Your letter of the 1st is before me and in the midst of a meeting I attempt to write a few [lines] to you though I have not much news to write, only that the devil is not dead in Salt Lake [City] if it is in Atkinville and the political pot is boiling and earth and hell are wishing to overthrow Zion but God reigns still and we have to trust in him. You may have read in the Herald an interview with the correspondent of the St. Lewis Democrat. But I want to say you must not believe all you read in the papers about what we say, for they do not tell the truth. They make us say a great deal we do not. My general health had been good this

---

[165] Presidents Wilford Woodruff, George Q. Cannon, and Joseph F. Smith toured LDS communities in the Pacific Northwest and western Canada Oct. 21–Nov. 16, 1889. Thomas G. Alexander, *Things in Heaven and Earth: The Life and Times of Wilford Woodruff, a Mormon Prophet* (Salt Lake City: Signature Books, 1991), 254.

winter except a cold in my lung which affected me a good deal.
Well I spent a month in going to Canada and returning with
G[eorge] Q C[annon], J[oseph] F S[mith], and B[righam] Young
[Jr]. We had a good time visiting the Saints. Saw a great country
full of rivers, mountains, forests, and prairies. Rivers full of fish.
Trout 1 to 25 lb. Salmon 5 to 40 lb. Pike from 1 to 50 lb. I caught 16
trout out of one hole in a few minutes. [Saw] the mountain sheep
and goats, [and] a grizzly, black, brown, and cinnamon bear. We
saw 10,000 geese and 5,000 ducks in one pond ¾ of a mile [long]
and ½ a mile wide but enough about that. My family are generally well except [that] Emma [Smith Woodruff] was taken deadly
sick a few nights since; she thought she was poisoned by eating
sardines from a can. She was very sick for 10 hours but finally got
relief. She was better this morning. All want to be remembered
to you and family. Remember me kindly to all. I hope you are all
doing well. As my mail is in I must stop writing.

> As ever yours
> W[ilford] Woodruff

LETTERS OF 1890

> Salt Lake City, Utah
> January 28, 1890

Elder William Atkin

Dear Brother

Your letter of the 20th inst. came duly to hand. I am very
sorry for the afflictions of Sister May [Atkin] and sincerely hope
she is much better before this and will soon be fully recovered
and I am pleased to hear that you and the most of your family

are enjoying fair health. The heavy damages done by the floods in the Rio Virgin are extremely lamentable but I hope the losses may in some measure be compensated [for] by the increased safety and facilities accruing from the new arrangements now in contemplation, for taking the water out farther up the stream. I understand a large amount of land will be brought under irrigation by the new canal, which should be awarded in some way to those whose lands have been washed away.

I hope you and your daughter[166] from Sanpete will enjoy a most pleasant and agreeable visit. And I would like very much to drop in to see you, but there seems very little prospect for any such an event happening very soon.

In regard to the "temple tank,"[167] I would like to know where it is located, and what are its dimensions? How long, and broad and deep? How many gallons of water it will hold and all the particulars—as I have not heard anything about it to my recollection. I suppose it is to be at or near the spring—or source of supply, but I would like you to tell me all about it, and what it will cost. It seems as though you were working at great disadvantage while the roads and weather are so bad.

I have got over my cold, and am enjoying very good health, but the pressure of the times feels like a heavy weight upon me. But we are in the hand of the Lord, and "he doeth all things well." May the Lord bless you and your family and all the saints is my prayer.

> With kind regards I am your brother
> W[ilford] Woodruff

---

[166] Rachel Violet Atkin (1861–1900), a daughter of William Atkin and Rachel Thompson: b. Mar. 14, 1861, in Salt Lake City; m. Swen Ole Nielson Feb. 14, 1878, in St. George; d. Oct. 26, 1900, in Fairview, Utah. Awerkamp, *Journal and Genealogies;* LDS Ancestral File.

[167] The temple tank was the water source for the LDS St. George Temple's subterranean font, where baptisms were to be performed by proxy on behalf of deceased ancestors and loved ones, as well as for the personal baptisms for St. George Stake members.

Salt Lake City, Utah
February 15, 1890

Elder William Atkin
Atkinville, Washington County

Dear Brother

Your letter of February 3rd came duly to hand. Press of business has prevented an earlier reply. It is gratifying to hear that your daughter May [Atkin] is so rapidly recovering from her illness, and that the other members of your family are all enjoying the inestimable blessing of good health. The tidings of the marriage of your son John [Atkin],[168] and of the prospective marriage of Joseph [Atkin][169] very soon, to two sisters,[170] is good. It is right and proper for the sons of Zion to marry the daughters of Zion, and through faithful, honorable and upright lives fulfil the measure of their creation and their destiny. I congratulate them and wish them continual prosperity and eternal happiness through fidelity to the cause of Zion.

I join you in hope that not many of our poor brethren will be great losers in the damage done by the late floods in the Rio Virgin, and that although the land which has been washed away is effectually lost to them, that they will make it up by getting land above, although they may have to expend their labor for it. Even that will be much better than no land at all in lieu of that washed away. My family are usually well. My own health is very

---

[168] John Peter Atkin (1867–94), a son of William Atkin and Rachel Thompson: b. Mar. 13, 1867, in Salt Lake City; m. Annie Walker Feb. 28, 1889, in St. George; d. Jan. 27, 1894, in St. George. Awerkamp, *Journal and Genealogies;* LDS Ancestral File.

[169] Joseph Thompson Atkin (1863–1938), a son of William Atkin and Rachel Thompson: b. June 21, 1863, in Salt Lake City; m. Eleanor Walker Dec. 3, 1884, in St. George; d. Aug. 11, 1938, in St. George. Awerkamp, *Journal and Genealogies;* LDS Ancestral File.

[170] John and Joseph Atkin (who were brothers) married Annie and Eleanor Walker (who were sisters).

good now, for which I am exceedingly thankful, although I took a slight cold yesterday, but I hope it won't amount to much.

Emma [Smith Woodruff] and her family are well and would send love if they knew I was.

President [George] Cannon is in the East, working for our cause against the powerful agencies now operating for the defilement of Zion. Surely Satan has great power and his struggles are desperate, knowing his time is short. But the kingdom of God will prevail and eventually triumph gloriously. Brother J[oseph] F S[mith] is where I can reach him when necessary, and although chafing somewhat in spirit at the condition of things, he is in no way visibly impaired by his long exilement.[171]

Your description of the temple tank and explanation of the manner of its construction are all I could wish, and the matter of your opinion in regard to the capacity of the lower end of the pipe, I think, is worthy of due consideration. It might be well for you to explain your views fully to President [John] McAllister and Brother [William] Thompson, and if they agree with you, let them bring the matter before us and we will give it attention.

With kind regards, your brother
W[ilford] Woodruff

Salt Lake City, Utah
March 18, 1890

William Atkin

Dear Brother

Your letter of February 22nd is before me and in reply concerning the piping I find there is in the bill sent 1,440 feet of

---

[171] Joseph F. Smith lived on the underground between 1884 and 1891 because of his practice of plural marriage. Garr et al., *Encyclopedia*, 1131.

1½ inch pipe and there is 1,020 feet of 2 inch pipe. [George] Ottinger[172] being acquainted and dealing in hydraulics thought that 1½ inch pipe would discharge as much water at the temple as 6 × 4½ × 3½ × 2½ inch would bring that distance. The only thing that I see that we can do is to supply the 1,440 feet of 1½ inch pipe with the same amount of 2 inch pipe. Of course we would have to send East for this which would take some time to get it to St. George. I expect to have another interview with Ottinger upon the subject. I am called to meeting so must close. See [William] Thompson's letter. Remember me to all your family.

As ever yours
W[ilford] Woodruff

Salt Lake City, Utah
April 2, 1890

Elder William Atkin
St. George

Dear Brother

Your letter of March 24th is before me. I have not had time to answer it before. In regard to the water question for the St. George Temple I wish to say, we have again consulted Brother [George] Ottinger and laid before him the views of Brother [William] Thompson and yourself; and he says that he will warrant that inch and a half pipe to deliver 435 gallons of water per minute, and that ought to satisfy us all. It is as much water as we will

---

[172] George Martin Ottinger (1833–1917), professor of art and volunteer fireman: b. Feb. 8, 1833, in Springfield, Penn.; m. Mary Jane Abbott McAllister Jan. 9, 1862, in Salt Lake City; d. Oct. 29, 1917, in Salt Lake City. Robert S. Olpin, *Dictionary of Utah Art* (Salt Lake City: Salt Lake Art Center in cooperation with the Utah American Revolution Bicentennial Commission, 1980), 172–81.

need; and I trust to his judgment, he being so well acquainted with hydraulics. I have written to Brother [John] McAllister and Brother Thompson upon this subject. I am glad you and your family are getting better. I had a very severe attack two days ago which lasted several hours, but through administering, etc. I was delivered. I feel alright today. My family are generally well. We are preparing for conference;[173] we expect a large company of people. A good share of the Quorum of the Twelve will be with us; and I hope we shall have a profitable time.

Of course you know our city is in the hands of the gentiles, and of course they will take advantage of us in every respect they can; but we have to trust in God. As I am very busy today I can only write a short letter. Remember me kindly to your family and inquiring friends. God bless you all.

Your brother in the gospel
W[ilford] Woodruff

Salt Lake City, Utah
April 26, 1890

Dear Brother and Sister Atkin

Now Brother William I am not going to address you alone and leave Sister [Rachel Thompson] Atkin out who has cooked for me for a year as I tell you we have got to acknowledge our wives or we will be in a bad fix. I have ate at your table for something like a year with Sister [Atkin] at the head to serve us and I think we would have been bad off without her so I must acknowledge her as the lady of the home who has done me and my family many kindnesses. I cannot forget the many

---

[173] The Sixtieth Annual LDS Church Conference was held in Salt Lake City, Apr. 4–6, 1890.

kindnesses and hours of comfort I have received in that stone
room built for my benefit and I would like to spend a few more
hours there if I had a chance. Well give my love and blessing to
Sister Atkin. Alice [Woodruff] had just come in and says give
my love to Nellie [Atkin] and May [Atkin]. She cannot forget
her romping with the girls over the hills. She says tell May to
eat a quail for her. She is now 11 years old. Attends school parties etc. and [acts] as girlish as ever. I suppose I am getting to be
an old man. I begin to feel a little more like [— —] than I did
when I took my gun at your home and went to the pond to shoot
some ducks or quails or a cottontail. I feel a little more stiffened
up than I did then. But I am so overwhelmed with meetings,
business, and care and [a] great deal of it of great magnitude and
personal interviews with hundreds upon almost every subject
imaginable that it makes my brain ache. My office is crowded
from morning till night and generally when I leave at night the
office is still crowded and I have to ride 3 miles to the farm to get
a little fresh air and rest. Now I expect there is a great change
at Atkinville since the flood. I am sorry it has taken off so much
of your land. I hope it has left you your levies and ponds for that
would be a great loss to you. Well Brother Atkin we are living
in strange times and passing a strange part of our history. Salt
Lake City is now in the hands of the gentiles and an illiterate
mob who are calculating to drive the Mormons out by taxation:
only think of my Valley House, taxed last year at $14,000 and
this year at $100,000 and the tax will be from $2,000 to $2,500
dollars, and so all the Mormon property will be taxed. The liberals stole the city and they intend to steal the county and Territory but they are in the hands of God as well as ourselves and
it seems as though the whole government were determined to
take away every right the Mormons possess but there they will
ripen the nation for just judgments of God and if the wicked
bring tribulation upon the Saints the wicked will not escape the

just judgments of God in their turn. Brother Atkin I am about to start upon a journey to visit Mexico with my councilors to organize the Saints in that land into a stake. I expect we will be gone a month. We will have to travel a good deal by wagon in that land which will be rather hard upon me but of course the main travel will be by railroad. Concerning our piping for the temple, we will have to determine what goes through a 6 inch pipe at the head—whether it takes a longer or shorter time— but I hope it will be successful. Emma [Smith Woodruff] and Owen [Woodruff] both expect to go with me to Mexico to take care of me the best they can and see the country. Emma joins me in sending love to you both and all the family. I would like to see your flock of sheep. You did not say what number you have. You will have to get along with the shearing without me this year. I think I will have to close this letter for this time. You can take months to write me for I expect to be gone that length of time. I see the world is still full of liars. Nearly all the papers in the United States have said that I stated at the last conference there would be no more revelation in this church. But I suppose the first liar started and the rest followed.

I remain as ever your brother
W[ilford] Woodruff

Salt Lake City, Utah
June 3, 1890

William Atkin

Dear Brother

I received your letter last evening which I read with much interest. I think you have been very much blessed in your sheep husbandry considering the amount of wool and lambs realized.

Was very much pleased to hear that Sister [Rachel Thompson] Atkin and the family were well, and was sorry to learn that you are having so much trouble with the flood, and losing so much of your land. I hope your pond will be preserved to you that your family may continue to be furnished with chub and carp. All the family were very glad to hear from you. We did not take the Mexican trip as Brother [George] Cannon had to leave for Washington; whether we will have time to visit Mexico or not this fall I do not know. My family are all generally well. As for myself I feel that time tells upon me, in a measure. I have very little time for rest; am very much crowded in the variety of our church business. I should like to come down and spend a few weeks with you if I had the time to visit my old tramping ground. Concerning affairs here, of course you know that our city is in the hands of the Philistines who call themselves "Liberals"; and apparently their intention is to tax all Mormons so that they will be obliged to sell their property or sell it for them for taxes. Our affairs at Washington are still unsettled. There has been great exertion made to hinder the passage of those infamous measures proposing the taking away of the rights of the people, but how it will result time must determine. Of course you know of the decision of the Supreme Court of the United States affecting our church property;[174] this, however, in part is still not entirely disposed of but will be I suppose after the summer vacation. We are having a good deal of rain this spring; had quite a rain, hail and snow storm yesterday. We are only just beginning to cut our first crop of lucerne; all crops look well. I received a letter from Brother [William] Thompson about laying water pipes for the

---

[174] On May 19, 1890, the U.S. Supreme Court ruled against the LDS Church in *The Late Corporation of the Mormon Church v. United States,* stating that the seizing of LDS Church property was legal under the Edmunds-Tucker Act. Ludlow, *Encyclopedia of Mormonism,* 1:53.

temple some time ago, but have not heard how they are getting along with that work of late. Emma [Smith Woodruff] and all the family wish to be remembered to you and family.

> As ever your brother in the gospel
> W[ilford] Woodruff

Salt Lake City, Utah
July 22, 1890

Elder William Atkin

Dear Brother

I have received your 2 letters, one of July 3rd and the other of [July] 15th. Of course, I am glad to hear from you. I have just returned from a journey of two weeks in the mountains. I came home almost a cripple, having broken a blood vessel in my right leg, which lames me for the time being.

Now concerning our waterworks. It seems that there has been quite a mistake in the expectation of that piping. I have heard nothing at all from Brother [John] McAllister on the subject. I do not know yet what will be done in the matter.

My family are well as usual. I had Emma [Smith Woodruff], Blanch [Woodruff], and Owen [Woodruff] with me in the mountains. We spent our time in camp; did considerable fishing in the Weber River;[175] caught some 200 trout. I did not catch a great many myself, because it was too hard to follow the stream, but of course that is all the good it did, so far as stopping him was concerned. He represented him as a very large animal. We

---

[175] The Weber River in northern Utah flows northwest from the western Uinta Mountains into the Great Salt Lake. It was named after a Dutch trapper, John H. Weber, who was killed by American Indians near the river in 1823. Van Cott, *Utah Place Names*, 392.

got a few chickens, which was all the game we secured, except-
ing killing a dozen porcupines.

Brother [Daniel] Wells and [Moses] Farnsworth were in this
morning from Manti, but being busy with other parties I did
not speak to them. I expect they will call again. Remember me
kindly to Sister [Rachel Thompson] Atkin and all the family.

As ever, your brother
W[ilford] Woodruff

Salt Lake City, Utah
September 1, 1890

William Atkin

Dear Brother

Just as I was about to start on a journey to Colorado and New
Mexico of some 2,500 miles I received your letter of August 4th.
I have had no time to answer it. We were called rather suddenly,
all of us. The 3 presidents[176] took cars [and] rode to Denver;[177]
on the way, [we] saw the Platte River[178] and were dined at
Laramie,[179] [then] went to Albuquerque,[180] where we met with
all the presidents of stakes in Arizona [and] gave them such
counsel as we thought best. We visited Santa Fe,[181] the oldest

---

[176] The three members of the LDS First Presidency at this time were Wilford Woodruff,
George Q. Cannon, and Joseph F. Smith.

[177] Denver, the capital city of Colorado, is in the northeastern part of Colorado on the South
Platte River. The city was founded by gold prospectors in 1860.

[178] The North Platte River is a tributary of the Platte River, which flows through Colorado,
Wyoming, and western Nebraska, where it merges with the South Platte River and then
flows into the Missouri River.

[179] Laramie, a city in Albany County in southeastern Wyoming, was settled in 1868.

[180] Albuquerque, a city in Bernalillo County in central New Mexico, was founded in 1706.

[181] Santa Fe, the capital city of New Mexico, is in north-central New Mexico. Founded by
the Spanish in 1609–10, it is one of the oldest European settlements in the United States
but not the oldest.

city in America. The oldest cathedral, oldest house, and oldest bell—all of which we visited. The bell was cast in 1370 [and was] brought from Spain. One day we traveled 40 miles in [a] carriage. We attended the conference of Manassa.[182] Silas S. Smith[183] [is] president. We returned home [and] found half a bushel of letters. Stayed one day in the office then went 70 miles to Skull Valley.[184] Went and met with the Islanders.[185] Held meeting with them. Gone 4 days and returned home; have our office full but [I] steal a moment to answer this letter. My health is about as usual; all say I look well and most of the time [I] feel well. Our brethren are in court today testifying upon church property. Give my love to all of the family.

As ever I remain yours
W[ilford] Woodruff

Private. Look out for croakers; the courts are after more property.

---

[182] Manassa is a town in Conejos County in south-central Colorado. Settled by Mormon pioneers in 1879, it was named after the son of Old Testament patriarch Joseph (Israel). It was the headquarters of the San Luis Stake, organized in 1883. Jenson, *Encyclopedic History*, 467–68.

[183] Silas Sanford Smith (1830–1910), president of the LDS San Luis Stake, 1883–92: b. Oct, 26, 1830, in Stockholm, N.Y., to Silas Smith and Mary Aikens; m. Clarinda Ann Ricks July 9, 1851, in Layton, Utah; d. Oct, 11, 1910, in Layton. Jenson, *Biographical Encyclopedia*, 1:801–802; LDS Ancestral File.

[184] Skull Valley is a broad expanse of land between the Stansbury and Onaqui mountains in Tooele County in northern Utah. Settled by Mormon pioneers, it was named Skull Valley after the prehistoric buffalo skulls found there in 1853–54. Van Cott, *Utah Place Names*, 343.

[185] Between 1889 and 1916, LDS converts from Hawaii were encouraged to settle in Skull Valley, where they could be closer to LDS temples in Utah. Their colony was named Iosepa (Hawaiian for Joseph) in honor of Joseph Smith and Joseph F. Smith. Van Cott, *Utah Place Names*, 200.

Salt Lake City, Utah
October 23, 1890

William Atkin

Dear Brother

Your letter of October 4th was received. I signed your recommends and forwarded them to you, which I hope you received. We are still in the woods as far as hard work is concerned, and I don't know when we shall get out. I have no particular news to write you. I am well as usual, so is my family. Robert Scholes[186] has been here on a visit, and has just returned. Susan [Woodruff Scholes] was here also, and returned yesterday. She has one daughter sick with diphtheria,[187] which hastened her return. All is well.

As ever yours,
W[ilford] Woodruff

Salt Lake City, Utah
November 19, 1890

Dear Brother William

In looking over my package of letters I see one from you of September 25th that is not marked answered so I judge I have not answered it. It is quite an interesting letter in many respects. I would be very glad to join you in melons and pears and would enjoy a dinner of carp with Sister [Rachel Thompson] Atkin for

---

[186] Robert Scholes (1835–91), a son-in-law of Wilford Woodruff and Phoebe Whittemore Carter: b. Nov. 19, 1835, in Manchester, England, to George Scholes and Maria Whitehead; m. Susan Cornelia Woodruff Jan. 30, 1859; d. July 14, 1891, in Sioux City, Iowa. Jackson, *Wilford Woodruff Family;* LDS Ancestral File.

[187] Diphtheria is a contagious disease caused by bacterium that produces irritation of the heart and nervous system.

I know what her cooking is; she has had a long experience in that line with a full table. I am as busy as ever and enjoying fair health today. I was confined to my room a week with a severe cold on my lungs. I was quite pleased to learn that you had such a good flock of sheep. They are quite a profitable stock where a person can take care of them. I am glad your enemies do not trouble you and that you have no *fault* to *find* with *yourself* and if you don't I am sure your neighbors will have no cause to. I have had quite a visit from Robert and Susan [Woodruff] Scholes. Robert looks quite young and well. Susan wanted to stay in Utah and not go home but she got a telegram that her daughter Eliza [Scholes] was quite sick with diphtheria. She took the car and got home before Robert did. We still have friends and foes. I have been trying to go to Mexico with my councilor to organize a stake but [have] not got to it. Give my love and blessings to your wife and children. I enclose with this one of my *Manifestos*.[188]

> I remain your
> Wilford Woodruff

[188] The Manifesto was an official statement issued by President Wilford Woodruff on September 24, 1890, which declared an end to future plural marriages by Latter-day Saints; it was later canonized by church members as Official Declaration 1 in the Doctrine and Covenants (see appendix 3). Garr et al., *Encyclopedia*, 699–701.

APPENDIX I

Wilford Woodruff Chronology

March 1, 1807	Born in Avon, Hartford County, Connecticut, to Aphek Woodruff and Beulah Thompson Woodruff
December 31, 1833	Baptized in Richland, New York, by Zera Pulsipher
April 25, 1834	Arrives in Kirtland, Ohio, headquarters of Mormon Church
May 1, 1834	Departs for Missouri with Zion's Camp
June 28, 1835	Ordained elder in LDS Church in Benton County, Tennessee, by Warren Parrish
May 31, 1836	Ordained a Seventy in LDS Church and sealed to eternal life by David W. Patten and Warren Parrish
April 13, 1837	Marries Phoebe W. Carter, ceremony performed by Frederick G. Williams
April 15, 1837	Receives patriarchal blessing by Joseph Smith, Sr.
May 31, 1837	Departs on mission to Maine with Jonathan Hale and Milton Holmes
July 1, 1838	Baptizes father, mother, and sister in Farmington, Connecticut
August 9, 1838	Receives call to Mormon apostleship and mission to England

Adapted from Susan Staker, ed., *Waiting for the World's End: The Diaries of Wilford Woodruff* (Salt Lake City: Signature Books, 1993), xxiii–xxxviii.

April 26, 1839	Ordained apostle by Brigham Young in Far West, Missouri
July 22, 1839	Witnesses Joseph Smith healing sick at Commerce (later Nauvoo), Illinois
August 8, 1839	Departs on mission to England with John Taylor
January 11, 1840	Arrives in Liverpool, England
October 6, 1841	Arrives in Nauvoo, Illinois
February 3, 1842	Appointed business manager of *Times and Seasons*
November 11, 1843	Sealed for eternity to Phoebe Carter Woodruff by Hyrum Smith
December 2, 1843	Receives Holy Order endowment with Parley P. Pratt, Orson Hyde, George A. Smith, and Orson Spencer
May 9, 1844	Leaves Nauvoo on political mission
July 9, 1844	Learns of martyrdom of Joseph Smith
August 28, 1844	Leaves with Phoebe to preside over British Mission
January 23, 1846	Leaves England
May 22, 1846	Leaves Nauvoo to join Iowa encampment, eventually settling in Winter Quarters on banks of Mississippi River
April 7, 1847	Pioneer company leaves Winter Quarters
July 24, 1847	Enters Great Salt Lake valley
December 5, 1847	First Presidency reorganized with Brigham Young, Heber C. Kimball, and Willard Richards
June 21, 1848	Leaves for Boston to preside over church in eastern states and Canada
February 3, 1851	Weekly meetings of Twelve begin; given charge of official records of the Twelve Apostles

December 21, 1852	Appointed clerk and historian of Twelve Apostles
February 14, 1853	Attends groundbreaking ceremony for Salt Lake temple site
May 5, 1855	Attends dedication of Endowment House
April 7, 1856	Appointed assistant church historian and superintends work in absence of George A. Smith
July 24, 1857	Word arrives of expedition of U.S. Army to administer federal law in territory
August 17, 1858	Federal troops enter Salt Lake Valley
November 5, 1860	Elected to fill Orson Pratt's seat in Utah legislature
August 22, 1863	Predicts building of Logan Temple
October 7, 1866	First meeting in new Salt Lake Tabernacle
December 2, 1867	School of the Prophets reinstituted
March 1, 1869	Zion's Cooperative Mercantile Institution (zcmi) dedicated
October 25, 1869	William S. Godbe, E. L. T. Harrison, and Eli B. Kelsey excommunicated for economic dissent and spiritualism
September 9, 1872	Departs for California State Fair
February 14, 1873	U.S. Congress debates antipolygamy legislation but fails to pass
April 10, 1875	Seniority adjusted in Quorum of Twelve; John Taylor and Wilford placed before Orson Hyde and Orson Pratt
January 1, 1877	Dedicates portions of St. George Temple
January 10, 1877	With Brigham Young administers first ordinances in St. George Temple
August 21, 1877	Baptized for signers of Declaration of Independence

August 29, 1877	Brigham Young dies
February 7, 1879	Begins life "on the underground" to avoid arrest for bigamy
March 6, 1879	Departs for Arizona and New Mexico; spends rest of year there; works among American Indians
January 26, 1880	Receives wilderness revelation
October 9, 1880	First Presidency reorganized with George Q. Cannon and Joseph F. Smith as counselors to John Taylor; Woodruff sustained as president of Quorum of Twelve; John Henry Smith and Francis M. Lyman called to Twelve
December 19, 1880	Makes first telephone call
March 14, 1882	U.S. Congress passes antipolygamy Edmunds Act
April 20, 1882	U.S. House of Representatives refuses to seat First Presidency counselor George Q. Cannon
May 17, 1884	Logan Temple dedicated
November 10, 1885	Phoebe W. Carter Woodruff dies
February 8, 1886	Narrow escape from U.S. marshals
February 14, 1886	Apostle George Q. Cannon arrested
January 13, 1887	Antipolygamy Edmunds-Tucker Act passes U.S. House of Representatives
February 19, 1887	Edmunds-Tucker Act passes U.S. Senate
July 25, 1887	President John Taylor dies
May 17, 1888	Manti Temple dedicated
July 9, 1888	Court-appointed receiver negotiates confiscation of church property
September 17, 1888	Apostle Cannon begins 175-day prison term for unlawful cohabitation
April 7, 1889	Sustained as president of church with George Q. Cannon and Joseph F. Smith as counselors

April 13–26, 1889	Excursion to San Francisco and Monterey, California
November 24, 1889	Receives revelation on politics and polygamy
May 19, 1890	U.S. Supreme Court upholds Edmunds-Tucker Act
August 11–24, 1890	Tour of Wyoming, Colorado, New Mexico, and Arizona
September 24, 1890	Manifesto ending plural marriage issued
May 9, 1891	U.S. president William H. Harrison visits
October 25, 1891	Defense of Manifesto and testimony
April 6, 1893	Salt Lake Temple dedicated
August 29, 1893	Excursion to Chicago World's Fair
December 13, 1893	Utah statehood approved
July 17, 1894	U.S. president Grover Cleveland signs Utah enabling act
January 4, 1896	Utah statehood celebrated
April 6, 1896	Political Manifesto issued
September 2, 1898	Dies in San Francisco

The Families of Wilford Woodruff and William Atkin

The Wives and Children of Wilford Woodruff (1807–1898)

Phoebe Whittemore Carter (1807–1885)
    Sarah Emma Woodruff (1838–1840)
    Wilford Woodruff, Jr. (1840–1921)
    Phoebe Amelia Woodruff (1842–1919)
    Susan Cornelia Woodruff (1843–1897)
    Joseph Woodruff (1845–1846)
    Ezra Woodruff (1846–1846)
    Sarah Carter Woodruff (1847–1848)
    Beulah Augusta Woodruff (1851–1905)
    Aphek Woodruff (1853–1853)

Mary Ann Jackson (1818–1894)
    James Jackson Woodruff (1847–1927)

All Woodruff family naming conventions and biographical data are taken from Ronald Vern Jackson, *Wilford Woodruff Family* (Bountiful, Utah: Accelerated Indexing Systems, 1980); and LDS Family Search Ancestral File (database available at www.familysearch.org). All Atkin family naming conventions and biographical data are taken from Jacqueline Williams Awerkamp, *William Atkin and Rachel Thompson Journal and Genealogies* (n.p.: privately published, 1976); and LDS Family Search Ancestral File.

Mary Carolyn Barton (ca. 1829–?)
  No children

Mary Giles Meeks Webster (1803–1852)
  No children

Emma Smoot Smith (1838–1912)
  Hyrum Smith Woodruff (1857–1858)
  Emma Minilla Woodruff (1860–1905)
  Asahel Hart Woodruff (1863–1939)
  Ann Thompson Woodruff (1867–1867)
  Clara Martina Woodruff (1869–1927)
  Abraham Owen Woodruff (1872–1904)
  Winnifred Blanch Woodruff (1875–1954)
  Mary Alice Woodruff (1879–1916)

Sarah Brown (1834–1909)
  David Patten Woodruff (1854–1936)
  Brigham Young Woodruff (1857–1877)
  Phoebe Arabella Woodruff (1859–1939)
  Sylvia Malvina Woodruff (1862–1940)
  Newton Woodruff (1863–1960)
  Mary Woodruff (1867–1913)
  Charles Henry Woodruff (1870–1871)
  Edward Randolph Woodruff (1873–1873)

Sarah Delight Stocking (1838–1906)
  Marion Woodruff (1861–1946)
  Emeline Woodruff (1863–1915)
  Ensign Woodruff (1865–1954)
  Jeremiah Woodruff (1868–1869)
  Rosanna Woodruff (1871–1872)
  John Jay Woodruff (1873–1964)
  Julia Delight Stocking Woodruff (1878–1954)

Eudora Lovina Young (1852–1922)
  Unnamed child (1878)

The Wife and Children of
William Atkin (1835–1900)

Rachel Thompson (1835–1903)
  Ester Ann Atkin (1857–1868)
  William Atkin, Jr. (1859–1941)
  Rachel Violet Atkin (1861–1900)
  Joseph Thompson Atkin (1863–1938)
  Henry Thomas Atkin (1865–1938)
  John Peter Atkin (1867–1894)
  George Alma Atkin (1870–1921)
  Heber Charles Atkin (1872–1942)
  Enoch Atkin (1874–1874)
  May Atkin (1877–1927)
  Hyrum Atkin (1879–1958)
  Nellie Martha Atkin (1882–1963)

1890 Manifesto Announcement (Doctrine and Covenants, Official Declaration 1)

To Whom It May Concern:

Press dispatches having been sent for political purposes, from Salt Lake City, which have been widely published, to the effect that the Utah Commission, in their recent report to the Secretary of the Interior, allege that plural marriages are still being solemnized and that forty or more such marriages have been contracted in Utah since last June or during the past year, also that in public discourses the leaders of the Church have taught, encouraged and urged the continuance of the practice of polygamy—

I, therefore, as President of the Church of Jesus Christ of Latter-day Saints, do hereby, in the most solemn manner, declare that these charges are false. We are not teaching polygamy or plural marriage, nor permitting any person to enter into its practice, and I deny that either forty or any other number of plural marriages have during that period been solemnized in our Temples or in any other place in the Territory.

One case has been reported, in which the parties allege that the marriage was performed in the Endowment House, in Salt Lake City, in the Spring of 1889, but I have not been able to learn who performed the ceremony; whatever was done in this matter was without my knowledge. In consequence of this alleged occurrence the Endowment House was, by my instructions, taken down without delay.

Inasmuch as laws have been enacted by Congress forbidding plural marriages, which laws have been pronounced constitutional by the court of last resort, I hereby declare my intention to submit to those laws, and to use my influence with the members of the Church over which I preside to have them do likewise.

There is nothing in my teachings to the Church or in those of my associates, during the time specified, which can be reasonably construed to inculcate or encourage polygamy; and when any Elder of the Church has used language which appeared to convey any such teaching, he has been promptly reproved. And I now publicly declare that my advice to the Latter-day Saints is to refrain from contracting any marriage forbidden by the law of the land.

Wilford Woodruff
President of the Church of
Jesus Christ of Latter-day Saints

President Lorenzo Snow offered the following:

"I move that, recognizing Wilford Woodruff as the President of the Church of Jesus Christ of Latter-day Saints, and the only man on the earth at the present time who holds the keys of the sealing ordinances, we consider him fully authorized by virtue of his position to issue the Manifesto which has been read in our hearing, and which is dated September 24th, 1890, and that as a Church in General Conference assembled, we accept his declaration concerning plural marriages as authoritative and binding."
The vote to sustain the foregoing motion was unanimous.
Salt Lake City, Utah, October 6, 1890.

Excerpts from three addresses by President Wilford Woodruff regarding the Manifesto:

The Lord will never permit me or any other man who stands as President of this Church to lead you astray. It is not in the programme. It is not in the mind of God. If I were to attempt that, the Lord would remove me out of my place, and so He will any other man who attempts to lead the children of men astray from the oracles of God and from their duty. (Sixty-first Semi-annual General Conference of the Church, Monday, October 6, 1890, Salt Lake City, Utah. Reported in *Deseret Evening News*, October 11, 1890, p. 2.)

It matters not who lives or who dies, or who is called to lead this Church, they have got to lead it by the inspiration of Almighty God. If they do not do it that way, they cannot do it at all. . . .

I have had some revelations of late, and very important ones to me, and I will tell you what the Lord has said to me. Let me bring your minds to what is termed the manifesto. . . .

The Lord has told me to ask the Latter-day Saints a question, and He also told me that if they would listen to what I said to them and answer the question put to them, by the Spirit and power of God, they would all answer alike, and they would all believe alike with regard to this matter.

The question is this: Which is the wisest course for the Latter-day Saints to pursue—to continue to attempt to practice plural marriage, with the laws of the nation against it and the opposition of sixty millions of people, and at the cost of the confiscation and loss of all the Temples, and the stopping of all the ordinances therein, both for the living and the dead, and the imprisonment of the First Presidency and Twelve and the heads of families in the Church, and the confiscation of personal property of the people (all of which of themselves would stop the practice); or, after doing and suffering what we have through our adherence to this principle to cease the practice and submit to the law, and through doing so leave the Prophets, Apostles and fathers at home, so that they can instruct the people and attend to the duties of the Church, and also leave the Temples in the hands of the Saints, so that they can attend to the ordinances of the Gospel, both for the living and the dead?

The Lord showed me by vision and revelation exactly what would take place if we did not stop this practice. If we had not stopped it, you would have had no use for . . . any of the men in this temple at Logan; for all ordinances would be stopped throughout the land of Zion. Confusion would reign throughout Israel, and many men would be made prisoners. This trouble would have come upon the whole Church, and we should have been compelled to stop the practice. Now, the question is, whether it should be stopped in this manner, or in the way the Lord has manifested to us, and leave our Prophets and Apostles and fathers free men, and the temples in the hands of the people, so that the dead may be redeemed. A large number has already been delivered from the prison house in the spirit world by this people, and shall the work go on or stop? This is the question I lay before the Latter-day Saints. You have to judge for yourselves. I want you to answer it for yourselves. I shall not answer it; but I say to you that that is exactly the condition we as a people would have been in had we not taken the course we have.

. . . I saw exactly what would come to pass if there was not something done. I have had this spirit upon me for a long time. But I want to say this: I should have let all the temples go out of our hands; I should have gone to prison myself, and let every other man go there, had not the God of heaven commanded me to do what I did do; and when the hour came that I was commanded to do that, it was all clear to me. I went before the Lord, and I wrote what the Lord told me to write. . . .

I leave this with you, for you to contemplate and consider. The Lord is at work with us. (Cache Stake Conference, Logan, Utah, Sunday, November 1, 1891. Reported in *Deseret Weekly,* November 14, 1891.)

Now I will tell you what was manifested to me and what the Son of God performed in this thing. . . . All these things would have come to pass, as God Almighty lives, had not that Manifesto been given. Therefore, the Son of God felt disposed to have that thing presented to the Church and to the world for purposes in his own mind. The Lord had decreed the establishment of Zion. He had decreed the finishing of this temple. He had decreed that the salvation of the living and the dead should be given in these valleys of the mountains. And Almighty God decreed that the Devil should not thwart it. If you can understand that, that is a key to it. (From a discourse at the sixth session of the dedication of the Salt Lake Temple, April 1893. Typescript of Dedicatory Services, Church History Library, Church of Jesus Christ of Latter-day Saints, Salt Lake City.)

Further Reading

WILFORD WOODRUFF FAMILY

Alexander, Thomas G. *Things in Heaven and Earth: The Life and Times of Wilford Woodruff, a Mormon Prophet*. Salt Lake City: Signature Books, 1991.

Gibbons, Francis M. *Wilford Woodruff: Wondrous Worker, Prophet of God*. Salt Lake City: Deseret Book, 1988.

Jackson, Ronald Vern. *Wilford Woodruff Family*. Bountiful, Utah: Accelerated Indexing Systems, 1980.

Woodruff, Wilford. *Wilford Woodruff, Fourth President of the Church of Jesus Christ of Latter-day Saints: History of His Life and Labors as Recorded in His Daily Journals*. Edited and compiled by Matthias F. Cowley. Salt Lake City: Deseret News, 1909.

———. *Wilford Woodruff's Journal, 1833–1898, Typescript*. Edited by Scott G. Kenney. 9 vols. Midvale, Utah: Signature Books, 1983–84.

WILLIAM AND RACHEL ATKIN FAMILY

Awerkamp, Jacqueline Williams. *William Atkin and Rachel Thompson Journal and Genealogies*. Privately printed, 1976.

Neilson, Reid L. *From the Green Hills of England to the Red Hills of Dixie: The Story of William and Rachel Thompson Atkin*. Provo, Utah: Red Rock Publishing, 2000.

———, ed. *Writings of William Atkin: A Youth's Experience and Handcart Experience*. Provo, Utah: Privately printed, 1999.

Woodbury, Grace Atkin, and Angus Munn Woodbury. *The Story of Atkinville: A One-Family Village*. Salt Lake City: Privately printed, 1957.

MORMON LEGAL AND POLITICAL HISTORY

Firmage, Edwin Brown, and Richard Collin Mangrum. *Zion in the Courts: A Legal History of the Church of Jesus Christ of Latter-day Saints, 1830–1900*. Urbana: University of Illinois Press, 1988.

Hansen, Klaus J. *Quest for Empire: The Political Kingdom of God and the Council of Fifty in Mormon History.* East Lansing: Michigan State University Press, 1967.

Hill, Marvin S. *Quest for Refuge: The Mormon Flight from American Pluralism.* Salt Lake City: Signature Books, 1989.

Lyman, E. Leo. *Political Deliverance: The Mormon Quest for Utah Statehood.* Urbana: University of Illinois Press, 1986.

Winn, Kenneth H. *Exiles in a Land of Liberty: Mormons in America, 1830–1846.* Chapel Hill: University of North Carolina Press, 1989.

MORMON POLYGAMY

Daynes, Kathryn M. *More Wives Than One: The Transformation of the Mormon Marriage System, 1840–1910.* Urbana: University of Illinois Press, 2001.

Embry, Jessie L. *Mormon Polygamous Families: Life in the Principle.* Salt Lake City: University of Utah Press, 1987.

Foster, Lawrence. *Religion and Sexuality: Three American Communal Experiments of the Nineteenth Century.* New York: Oxford University Press, 1981.

Hardy, B. Carmon, ed. *Doing the Works of Abraham: Mormon Polygamy; Its Origin, Practice, and Thought.* Norman, Okla.: Arthur H. Clark Company, 2007.

———. *Solemn Covenant: The Mormon Polygamous Passage.* Urbana: University of Illinois Press, 1992.

LIFE ON THE POLYGAMY "UNDERGROUND"

Alexander, Thomas G. "An Apostle in Exile: Wilford Woodruff and the St. George Connection." Juanita Brooks Lecture Series, 1994. St. George, Utah: Dixie College, 1994.

Cresswell, Stephan. "The U.S. Department of Justice in Utah Territory, 1870–1890." *Utah Historical Quarterly* 53 (Summer 1985): 204–22.

Larson, Andrew Karl. "Hare and Hounds: The Polygamy Raid." In A. Larson, *"I Was Called to Dixie": The Virgin River Basin, Unique Experiences in Mormon Pioneering,* 624–37. Salt Lake City: Deseret News Press, 1961.

Larson, Gustive O. "On the Underground" and "The Underground and the Visible Church." In G. Larson, *The "Americanization" of Utah for Statehood,* 155–82. San Marino, Calif.: Huntington Library, 1971.

Panek, Tracey E. "Search and Seizure in Utah: Recounting the Antipolygamy Raids." *Utah Historical Quarterly* 62 (Fall 1994): 316–34.

The 1890 Manifesto

Alexander, Thomas G. "The Odyssey of a Latter-day Prophet: Wilford Woodruff and the Manifesto of 1890." *Journal of Mormon History* 17 (1991): 169–206.

————. "Wilford Woodruff and the Changing Nature of Mormon Religious Experience." *Church History* 45 (March 1976): 50–69.

Godfrey, Kenneth W. "The Coming of the Manifesto." *Dialogue: A Journal of Mormon Thought* 5 (Autumn 1970): 11–25.

Lyman, E. Leo. "The Political Background of the Woodruff Manifesto." *Dialogue: A Journal of Mormon Thought* 24 (Fall 1991): 21–39.

Shipps, Jan. "The Principle Revoked: A Closer Look at the Demise of Plural Marriage." *Journal of Mormon History* 11 (1984): 65–77.

Contributors

DR. THOMAS G. ALEXANDER, Lemuel Harrison Redd Jr. Professor of Western American History Emeritus at Brigham Young University, is one of the leaders of the New Mormon History and a past president of the Mormon History Association. His books include *Mormonism in Transition: A History of the Latter-day Saints, 1890–1930; Things in Heaven and Earth: The Life and Times of Wilford Woodruff, a Mormon Prophet;* and *Utah, The Right Place: The Official Centennial History.*

DR. REID L. NEILSON, managing director of the Church History Department of The Church of Jesus Christ of Latter-day Saints, is a great-great-grandson of William and Rachel Thompson Atkin. He is the author of *From the Green Hills of England to the Red Hills of Dixie: The Story of William and Rachel Thompson Atkin,* as well as the author, editor, and coeditor of many books on Mormon history, including *Early Mormon Missionary Activities in Japan, 1901–1924* and *Joseph Smith Jr.: Reappraisals after Two Centuries.*

DR. JAN SHIPPS, a professor of history and religious studies emeritus at Indiana University–Purdue University Indianapolis, is one of the foremost scholars of Mormonism and a past president of the Mormon History Association. She is the author of *Mormonism: The Story of a New Religious Tradition* and *Sojourner in the Promised Land: Forty Years among the Mormons,* as well as the coeditor of *The Journals of William E. McLellin.*

Index

LDS Church, annual conferences: 1887, 145, 145n62; 1888, 165; 1889, 177–78; 1890, 189, 189n173; Woodruff in hiding during, 154, 154n92

LDS Church History Library, 15–16, 20, 23

LDS Church, leadership: acknowledgement of polygamy, 59; "Addy" as pseudonym, 162, 162n119; attitude toward women, 52n68; campaign for statehood, 69–73, 80–81, 95; encouragement of plural marriage, 51–52, 52n68; Manifesto acceptance, 95–96, 208; Manifesto interpretation, 117–24; relief from federal prosecution, 66–67; responding to government sanctions, 87–93; sharing politics with non-Mormons, 82–87, 92, 94–96; succession following Taylor's death, 64–66; temple and stake changes, 169–70; Woodruff as president, 14–15, 96; Woodruff positions of, 12, 80. *See also* First Presidency; Quorum of the Twelve Apostles; Smith, Joseph; Taylor, John; Young, Brigham

LDS Church, temples/temple dedications: Logan Temple, 62, 73, 202; Manti Temple, 62, 156–57, 160, 202; Nephi Temple, 178; Salt Lake City Temple, 55, 132, 180n160; St. George Temple, 31, 202

LDS Doctrine and Covenants, 41, 41n32

Letters of Wilford Woodruff: discovery of, 15, 127n3; editorial method for, 21–24, 57n1; genealogical abbreviations, 127n2; historical importance, 12, 16–17; place-names, 127n1; post-Manifesto communications, 53–56; written in 1885, 127–32; written in 1887, 132–49; written in 1888, 149–70; written in 1889, 171–84; written in 1890, 184–97. *See also* letters by year

Liberal (gentile) Party: known as "the

ring," 151, 169, 179, 179n157; role in immigration politics, 75; role in loyalty politics, 77; in Salt Lake City politics, 82, 84–87, 113, 192; in territorial politics, 83n70–71, 84, 151n82. *See also* People's (LDS) Party

Lipman, Joseph, 75

Little Cottonwood Canyon, 179, 179nn159–60

Little Gold Pieces (Jensen), 117

Logan, Ephraim, 135n35

Logan, Utah, 73, 135, 135n35

Logue, Larry M., 52

Lyman, Amasa M. and Maria Louisa Tanner, 173n143

Lyman, Francis Marion, 67, 173, 173n143

Lyman, Rhoda Ann Taylor, 173n143

MacDonald, A. F., 73n43

Madsen, Caroline Jensen, 166n126

Madsen, Mads Peterson and Mette Marie, 166n126

Madsen, Peter, 166, 166n126

Manifest of the Apostles, 79–80

Manifesto of 1890: acceptance of, 120–21, 208; as divine revelation, 16–17; full text of, 207–208; impact on women, 117–21; interpretation and division over, 115–17; issuance of, 14, 53, 57–58, 91–92, 113; issuance of Second Manifesto, 121; as Official Declaration, 58, 197n188; revelations leading to, 59–61, 61n10; Woodruff addresses explaining, 209–11; Woodruff letters following, 53–56. *See also* LDS Church, leadership; Patriarchal order of marriage

Manifesto of the Apostles of 1889, 79–80, 95–96

Manassa, Colo., 195, 195n182

Manti, Utah, 156, 156n94

Manti Temple, 156, 156n95, 159n105

Marriage. *See* Patriarchal order of marriage